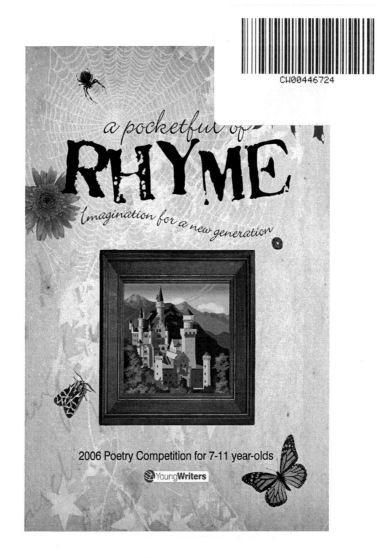

CW00446724

a pocketful of
RHYME
Imagination for a new generation

2006 Poetry Competition for 7-11 year-olds
YoungWriters

UK Verses Vol IV
Edited by Young Writers

First published in Great Britain in 2006 by:
Young Writers
Remus House
Coltsfoot Drive
Peterborough
PE2 9JX
Telephone: 01733 890066
Website: www.youngwriters.co.uk

SB ISBN 1 84602 453 6

Foreword

Young Writers was established in 1991 and has been passionately devoted to the promotion of reading and writing in children and young adults ever since. The quest continues today. Young Writers remains as committed to the nurturing of poetic and literary talent as ever.

This year's Young Writers competition has proven as vibrant and dynamic as ever and we are delighted to present a showcase of the best poetry from across the UK and in some cases overseas. Each poem has been selected from a wealth of *A Pocketful Of Rhyme* entries before ultimately being published in this, our fourteenth primary school poetry series.

Once again, we have been supremely impressed by the overall quality of the entries we have received. The imagination, energy and creativity which has gone into each young writer's entry made choosing the poems a challenging and often difficult but ultimately hugely rewarding task - the general high standard of the work submitted ensured this opportunity to bring their poetry to a larger appreciative audience.

We sincerely hope you are pleased with this final collection and that you will enjoy *A Pocketful Of Rhyme UK Verses Vol IV* for many years to come.

Contents

Emily Ablett (10)	19
Holly Pegnam-Mason (9)	20
Demi-Lea Corr (8)	20
Devon Wright (9)	21
Bradley Woods (8)	21
Hannah Morse (9)	22
Emma Duxbury (9)	23
Jordan Wilcock (9)	24
Natalie Forshaw (9)	25
Danielle Parker (8)	26
Ben Murphy (9)	27
Rebecca Retford (9)	28
Lauren Nolan (9)	29
Laura Astley (9)	30
Lucy Boughey (8)	30
Gabby Hoinville (10)	31
Louis Pickering (9)	32

St Mary's Primary School, Enniskillen

Luachra Scott (7)	32
Oran McCarney (6)	33
Conor McCutcheon (6)	33

St Nicholas' CE Primary School, Liverpool

Lucy Seddon (10)	33
Alastair Cawdron (10)	34
Patrick Clarke (11)	34
Shaun Billows (11)	35
Michael Bowyer (11)	35
Jessica Wilson (10)	36
Ruth Cawdron (10)	36
Heather Cunningham (10)	37
Abbey Jones (10)	37
Georgina Fox (11)	38
Jessica Louise Fenlon (10)	38
Jamie Riley Hickey (11)	39
Sarah Leedham (11)	39
Joseph Duff (10)	40
Sarah Baden (10)	40
Melissa Wilding (10)	41

Katherine Weaver (8)	58
Chloe Broom (8)	58
Ella Benson (9)	59
Niamh Johnson (8)	59
Marina Godin (8)	59
Bethany Grace (8)	60
Sam Leverton (9)	60
Sean Lawes (8)	60
Christian Mortimer (9)	61
Thomas Hemingway (8)	61
Matthew Younger (8)	61
Kieran Borchard (9)	62
Rebecca Griffith (9)	62
Megan Kenyon (9)	62
Ben Longbottom-Smith (11)	63
James Bennison (9)	63
Mahala Woodhouse (10)	64
Connor McAlister-Payne (9)	65
Jonathan Korcu (9)	65
Nicole Leaver (9)	66
Kassie Morris (8)	66

Seamer & Irton CP School, Scarborough

Class BW (9/10)	67
Class PC (8/9)	68
Class LC (10/11)	69

Settle Primary School, Settle

Jessica Edwards (9)	69
Danielle Milner (10)	70
Emma Louise Leeming (9)	70
Grace McSharry (8)	70
Rosie Ralph (9)	71
Joe Bennison (9)	71
Molly Riley (8)	72
Laura Whorton (9)	72
Jacob Dryden (9)	73
Bethany Kate Fell	73
Alex Peter Tarbox (9)	74
George Gowland (8)	74
Elliott Lee (8)	74

Hugh Francmanis (8)	74
Jack Horsfall (8)	75
Steven Capstick (8)	75
Cameron Brook (7)	75
Shannon Louise Shortreed (8)	75
Louis Connor Gill (8)	76
Holly Mae Thornton (8)	76
Sam Laycock (8)	77
Kieran Illingworth (8)	77
Rowan Ashley Carpenter (8)	78
Lauren Smith (9)	78
Robert Adam Scaife (7)	78
Erin Scarlet Cokell (7)	79
Tara McManus (8)	79
Michael Chapman (9)	79
Alice Jane Syms (7)	80

South Milford CP School, Leeds

Nathan Moore (10)	80
Nick Jones (11)	81
Jack Baddon (10)	81
Billy Cheng (10)	82
Harrie Mosey (11)	82
Emilia Fuisdale (11)	83
Luke Rowling (11)	83
Beatrice Mills (11)	84
Beth Marchant (10)	85
Samuel Bryan (10)	86
Siân Harrison (10)	86
Hayley Lewis (11)	87
Sean Arron Stubbs (10)	87
Siobhan Wragg (10)	88
Matt Wilkinson (10)	88
Katie Buckthorpe (11)	89

Sutton-Upon-Derwent CE Primary School, York

Patrick Armitage (11)	89
Elizabeth Gray (10)	90
Sam Holme (11)	90
Ryan Bailey (11)	90
Megan Burrow (7)	91

Jon-Ross Richardson (7)   91
Jake Dunn (9)   91
Lauren Gill (8)   92
Alex Draycott (8)   92
Gemma Burrow (10)   92
Bethany Warren (8)   93
Megan Letts (9)   93

Valewood Primary School, Crosby
Ross Houlihan (8)   94
Sally Hayes-May (9)   94
Olivia Yoxall (9)   94
Nicola Smeaton (9)   95
Felipe Davis-Guzman (8)   95
Stephanie Taylor (9)   95
Max Forden (8)   96

Westholme Middle School, Blackburn
Charly Redmond (11)   96
Alice Holland (10)   96
Holly Adamson (11)   97
Charlotte Stockwell (11)   97
Heather Duckworth (10)   98
Malini Dey (10)   98
Lucy Janus (10)   99
Martha Hindle (10)   99
Klara Holmes (10)   100
Abigail Hindley (10)   101
Lauren Waterhouse (10)   102
Lydia Sage (10)   102
Melissa Duffy (10)   103
Laura Meredith Hallam (10)   103
Gabrielle Lamoury (10)   104
Rosie Hewson-Jones (9)   104
Amy Panchoo (11)   105
Emily Wright (7)   105
Zyra Shah (11)   106
Georgina Butler (10)   107
Eleanor Lynch (11)   108
Bronwyn Richards (8)   109
Salonee Shah (7)   110

The Poems

Jack Frost And The Snowman

I am Jack Frost,
I'll freeze you solid this year,
I'm as white as snow,
I'm as cold as ice,
I will definitely freeze you this winter.

I have two coal-black eyes,
I have an orange carrot nose,
I have a button mouth,
I have some buttons on my tummy,
I have stick arms,
I have a black hat,
I am a snowman.

Aisling Gray (9)
St Columban's Primary School, Belcoo

This Magical Kingdom!

In a beautiful land far away,
Where fairies and pixies lay,
Magical beasts and trolls
And dwarves dance around poles.

In a sparkling palace,
Gnomes party in lace,
Dragons nest in mountainsides,
Whilst the early bird slides.

The families give their garden a hoe,
As trees say hello,
In such a friendly fashion,
That everyone has a passion,
For this magical kingdom.

Gemma Wood (10)
St Cuthbert's School, Harrogate

Moon

The moon is
Like
A shining
Disco ball hanging
From the sky
But when
The daylight
Comes you wave
Bye-bye.

The moon is like a crystal
Ball, spinning around
And fading away
In the distance.

The moon is
Like a white
Glistening feather
Falling from the
Dark midnight sky.

Becky Hall (8)
St Cuthbert's School, Harrogate

The Tramp

With some hanging out braces
And some untied laces,
With some mucky, filthy hands
And some old tin cans.

With some old manky hats
And some dead smelly rats,
With some park benches for beds
And some newspapers to cover heads.

Natasha Chappell (7)
St Cuthbert's School, Harrogate

The Moon

The moon is like a Cyclops's eye
Rising over the
Horizon
Looking at
Everyone.

The moon is like
A silver tomato
With black holes in it.

The moon is like
A disco ball
Dancing in the
Midnight
Sky.

Daniel Fletcher (9)
St Cuthbert's School, Harrogate

The Moon

The moon is like a
Silver
Tomato rising
Over the
Horizon.

The moon is like a
Party starting
At midnight.

The moon is like a
Giant ball
Of cheese.

Courtney Banner (9)
St Cuthbert's School, Harrogate

The Moon

The moon
Is like
A
Disco ball
Shining silver
In
The midnight
Sky.

The moon is
As
Frosty as a
Freezer.

The moon is
A
Cupcake with
White, fluffy
Frosting.

The moon is
A football gliding
Across
The midnight
Sky.

The moon is
Like
A lollipop
With no
Stick.

Lindsey Wilderman (8)
St Cuthbert's School, Harrogate

Moon

The moon
Is the
London Eye
Glistening
In the
Night sky
As the stars
Twinkle above.

The moon
Is like a
Disco ball
Starting
A late
Night disco.

The crescent moon
Slips
Through the
Night sky like a
Giant's toenail.

The moon
Is a
Man
With a
Glowing
Mouth, always happy
Never sad.

Hannah Chapman (9)
St Cuthbert's School, Harrogate

The Moon

The moon rises,
Upon the sleepy town,
Like a sudden shock,
Moonlight.

The moon gleams,
Beams freezing air,
Like a penguin's dinner,
Streets silver.

The moon hides
Behind the fluffy clouds,
Like an ice cream cone
Just made.

The moon sleeps,
Creeps beyond the glistening river,
Like a soccer ball heading for the goal,
The moon goes down.

The sun rises,
For the morning day,
Like a dolphin jumping
In the sea.

Katie Derham (8)
St Cuthbert's School, Harrogate

The Moon

The moon is like a giant piece of cheese,
The moon is a shining torch glooming in the dark,
The moon is like a tub of vanilla ice cream,
The moon is a clock that tells us the time at night.

Jade Tasker
St Cuthbert's School, Harrogate

The Moon

At midnight the big ball
Is like a disco ball
Spinning round
In the midnight sky.

The moon is like
A party starting
In the sky
Crescent moon
It looks like
A king-sized toenail
Falling in the sky
The moon looks like the
London Eye looking
Over the Earth
The moon slips
Dips into light.

Shane Turnbull (10)
St Cuthbert's School, Harrogate

Untitled

(Based on 'Down Behind the Dustbin' by Michael Rosen)

Down behind the dustbin
I met a bee called Bumble,
He said he wouldn't eat the nectar,
He wanted apple crumble.

Down behind the dustbin,
I met a rabbit called Hop,
He said he wouldn't eat the carrot,
He'd prefer green soup.

Down behind the dustbin,
I met a cat called Coffee
He said he wouldn't eat the Whiskas,
He'd rather have toffee.

Liam Stevenson (8)
St Kentigern's Catholic Primary School, Blackpool

Down Behind The Dustbin

(Based on 'Down Behind the Dustbin' by Michael Rosen)

Down behind the dustbin
I met a dog called Sam
He didn't want to eat the bone
He'd prefer bread and jam.

Down behind the dustbin
I met a cat called Meg
She said she didn't like sausages
She'd prefer some milk and bread.

Down behind the dustbin
I met a frog called Nute
He didn't like the bag of crisps
He'd prefer a bowl of fruit.

Down behind the dustbin
I met a boy called Reg
He said he didn't want the chips
He'd prefer a bag of veg.

Thomas Squirrell (9)
St Kentigern's Catholic Primary School, Blackpool

Untitled

(Based on 'Down Behind the Dustbin' by Michael Rosen)

Down behind the dustbin I met a dog called Sam
He said he wouldn't eat the bone
He'd much prefer bread and jam.

Down behind the dustbin I met a dog called Paris
She was very cute and fluffy with her boyfriend Harris.

Down behind the dustbin I met a dog called Pixie
She loves to dress as a fairy and likes her Weetabix.

Down behind the dustbin I met a dog called Crystal
She has lots of kind friends to shoot her with a water pistol.

Daisy-May Shane (8)
St Kentigern's Catholic Primary School, Blackpool

Jabberkitty

(Based on 'Jabberwocky' by Lewis Carroll)

'Twas silent and the soothing shore,
Did roll and rumble in the cove.
All fluffy were the polar bears
And the air was filled with love!

'Beware the Jabberkitty my girl!
The ears that hear,
The claws that scratch!
Beware the Lippy bird
And the timid Randerpatch!'

She took her woollen blade in hand,
Searching for the cat she sought.
So rested she by the flower tree
And sat a moment in thought.

And as she rested for a bit,
The Jabberkitty with scary purrs,
Came pouncing through the dark wood,
Preparing an evil curse!

Miaow, miaow and ow and ow,
The woollen sword went snicker-snack,
She left it there and with its hair,
She went her long way back.

'And hast thus slain the Jabbercat?
Come to my arms my gorgeous girl!
O wondrous day, olé, olé!'
He shouted as he twirled.

'Twas silent and the soothing shore,
Did roll and rumble in the cove.
All fluffy were the polar bears
And the air was filled with love!

Jessica Allen (10)
St Kentigern's Catholic Primary School, Blackpool

Jabberjabber

(Based on 'Jabberwocky' by Lewis Carroll)

'Twas the Star Wars and the deadly clones
Did shoot and dodge in the war,
All full strength were the Jedi knights
And the weak humans outrage.

'Beware the Empire my son!
The guns that shoot, the bombs that blow
Beware Darth Vader and shun
The furious small Yoda.'

He took his saber sword in hand
Long time he saw the evil foe he saw
So rested he by the machinery
And stood a while in thought.

And in vital thought he stood
The Emperor with his hands of flame
Came flying through the starry space
And muttered as he came.

One, two! One, two! And through and through
The vorpal saber sliced his head
He left it dead and with its head
He went jogging back.

'And have you killed the Emperor?
Come to me my fearless boy
Oh great day! Oh yes! Oh yeah!'
He chortled in his joy.

'Twas Star Wars and the deadly clones
Did shoot and dodge in the war
All full strength were the Jedi knights
And the weak humans outrage.

Thomas Southworth (11)
St Kentigern's Catholic Primary School, Blackpool

Jabber Oompah Loompa

(Based on 'Jabberwocky' by Lewis Carroll)

'Twas tasty and the creamy chocolate
Did glisten and melt in the pot;
All hot were the bubbles dropped
And the children who bought the lot.

'Beware the Oompah Loompa my friends!
The songs they sing, the hair of green!
Beware the dancing one, and run
The chocolate man!'

He took his cocoa beans in hand:
Long time the cocoa bean ran -
So rested he by the jelly bean tree
And stood awhile in heat.

And as in chocolate thought,
The jabber Oompah Loompa, with eyes of bean,
Came dashing through the edible wood
And licked his lips as he came!

Yum-yum! Yum-yum! And through and through
The cocoa bean went sizzle and crackle!
He left it dead, and with its head
Swelling up with beans.

'And hast thou slain the Jabber Oompah Loompa?
Come to my home and stay awhile!
Oh what a day! Hooray! Hooray!'
He danced in his joy.

'Twas tasty and the creamy chocolate
Did glisten and melt in the pot:
All hot were the bubbles dropped
And the children who bought the lot.

Natalie Worthington (11)
St Kentigern's Catholic Primary School, Blackpool

Babawockey

(Based on 'Jabberwocky' by Lewis Carroll)

'Twas morning for the kid will scream
Will hit you and pull you and toxicate the room.
All funny were the baby clothes
And the brothers and sisters that moaned and groaned.

'Beware the stench my son.
The fumes that kill, the nappy that reeks.
Beware the baby rattle in all
Noisiation! And the annoying baby bouncer.'

So he took his nappy and baby wipe
Long time for the kid bin wiped
So he rested a while by the bathroom sink
And stood around in thought.

And as in uffish thought he stood,
The Babawock with eyes of fun
Came crawling down the hallway floor
And giggled as it came!

One, two! One, two! And wipe and wipe
The baby wipe did the trick.
He left it crying and with its waste
He went running back.

'And hast thou tackled the Babawock?
Go to the bin my beamish boy
Smelliest day! Callooh! Callay!'
He shouted in his joy.

'Twas morning, for the kid will scream
Will hit you and pull you and toxicate the room;
All funny were the baby clothes
And brothers and sisters that moaned and groaned.

Liam Scott-Rattray (10)
St Kentigern's Catholic Primary School, Blackpool

Cinderella

She had worked hard by day and night,
Her clothes were rags,
She looked a terrible sight.

The fairy godmother came to say,
She waved her wand
And made her day,
A beautiful dress,
She gave her to wear,
The people at the ball,
Started to stare.

Poor Cinderella had a
Hard life,
Prince Charming wanted to
Make her his wife.

Katie Guest (9)
St Mary's Catholic Junior School, Newton-le-Willows

My Football Match

When I got up
I went downstairs
And got my football out
I knew this was going to be a tough match.

When I arrived at the pitch
It was quite muddy, very slushy
And there was a very big ditch
The other team were all wearing blue.

When the match started
I ran down the field
Me and my teammates all parted
Then I knew it would be a tough match.

Daniel Thomas (9)
St Mary's Catholic Junior School, Newton-le-Willows

The Magic Box

(Based on 'Magic Box' by Kit Wright)

I will put in my box . . .
The swipe of a dragon's fire,
A picture of my best friends,
A packet of chocolate.

I will put in my box . . .
Fizzy pop,
Clothes,
Shoes.

I will put in my box . . .
A picture of my friend,
A cup of tea or coffee,
A picture of my dog, Bess.

I will put in my box . . .
A bow
A pen and paper
Some crayons.

Rebecca Holleran (8)
St Mary's Catholic Junior School, Newton-le-Willows

Water

(In the style of Alfred Noyes)

Water can be hot, water can be cool,
You can find it in the sea, or in the swimming pool.
My mum uses water to wash the dirty dishes,
You might even find a well and have two or three wishes.
There is water in the river,
That might give you a shiver.

My mum doesn't like the pool,
So she sits on a stool.
While we laugh and play,
My mum goes away.
I really like the water,
Because I'm a cool daughter.

Ellie Georgiou (9)
St Mary's Catholic Junior School, Newton-le-Willows

What Animal Am I?

Walking through the jungle,
Looking kind of humble,
With stripes as thick as night,
We see a pair of eyes shining so bright,
Slowly crawling in the grass,
Its tail twitching so fast,
Its ears pricked up, it hears its prey,
Poor little zebra won't get away,
It lies low ready to pounce,
It can't wait to eat,
Sitting there all alone,
All around him lots of bones,
Now he's eaten, he's full as a gun,
Let's go for a sleep away from the sun.

The answer is a tiger.

Danielle Doughty (11)
St Mary's Catholic Junior School, Newton-le-Willows

Cinderella

Down in the basement there was a girl called Cinderella,
She was working hard searching for her perfect fella,
She had two sisters, a real pain just like blisters.

Then her sisters were invited to a ball,
It said there would be lots of stalls,
In front of Cinderella was a fairy,
It was very, very scary.

She made a horse and carriage for Cinderella,
She's going searching for her fella,
She had a dance with the prince,
She's been working ever since,
As you guessed she lived happily ever after.

Elisha Bowes (9)
St Mary's Catholic Junior School, Newton-le-Willows

The Magic Box

(Based on 'Magic Box' by Kit Wright)

I will put in the box . . .
The first smile of Alfie,
Two cans of cola and
Me, Mum and Dad on a beach that is sunny.

I will put in the box . . .
A picture of Cornwall,
My cat and
A man that is tall.

I will put in the box . . .
A time machine,
Damwad the bear and
My first Hallowe'en.

I will put in the box . . .
All of my toys,
All of my things and
A whole pile of noise.

Jessica Parry (8)
St Mary's Catholic Junior School, Newton-le-Willows

The Magic Box

Based on 'Magic Box' by Kit Wright)

I will put in the box . . .
The carved surface of my football,
The shape of my football top.

I will put in the box . . .
The fun of the PlayStation 2 and
The round edge of the games.

I will put in the box . . .
The buttons of the remote and the
4 right-angled gold frame of the family photo.

The box is brown with golden hinges and crystals,
Diamonds, emeralds and rubies on it.

Jake Swift (9)
St Mary's Catholic Junior School, Newton-le-Willows

Friends

Who are your best friends?
The people who have best recommends,
They always are full of laughs,
Even if school is full of staff,
They are there to cheer you up,
With every one of their pups.

We all have a best mate,
Who is patient and waits,
You should always make up with them,
Because they are worth a precious gem,
They support you,
Even when you're blue.

You should always be a great pal,
Because they might take you to a canal,
If you do not feel well,
A visit from them, shall make you feel swell,
If someone tries to split up your mate and you,
You should say, 'Go to Peru.'

Cathrine Scowcroft (10)
St Mary's Catholic Junior School, Newton-le-Willows

A Cold Night

Raining outside, I was going to bed,
Getting heavy, I was starting to dread!
I got on my pyjamas, which were warm and thick,
I grabbed my hot water bottle and filled it quick!
So I jumped into bed and warmed up my feet,
I thought the rain was turning into sleet!
There was thunder and lightning, rain and hail,
Suddenly the wind gave out a wail!
I pulled my covers right up to my chin,
I felt nice and warm because my bed I was in.
I was snug in my bed, counting sheep,
I woke in the morning from my snuggly sleep.

Katie Carine
St Mary's Catholic Junior School, Newton-le-Willows

A Magic Box

(Based on 'Magic Box' by Kit Wright)

I will put in the box . . .
A picture of my two rabbits
And some of my very special habits.

My PSP and games
And some friends' first and second names.

I will put in the box . . .
A tail of a fox
And a piece of an ox,
A brick of my house
And a tail of a mouse.

I will put in the box . . .
A pair of socks
And a person that knocks,
I will put in my favourite bike and pedals.

Alix Stubbs (8)
St Mary's Catholic Junior School, Newton-le-Willows

The Magic Box

(Based on 'Magic Box' by Kit Wright)

I will put in the box . . .
Yasmin's voice
And also a little tortoise.

I will put in the box . . .
My brother's braces,
When my stepdad starts his races.

I will put in the box . . .
My mum's socks,
So she will remember that I am an ox.

The box is big and bold,
Silver and gold.

Danielle Barker (8)
St Mary's Catholic Junior School, Newton-le-Willows

The Magic Box

(Based on 'Magic Box' by Kit Wright)

I will put in the box . . .
The swish of a red magic top,
The drink of health that is pop,
The hat of a cop.

I will put in the box . . .
Santa's big black bag,
A magic paper that has a zag,
My sister's big nag.

My box is fashioned with steel that is silver and gold,
My box is big and bold,
The hinges are lined with noses that are cold.

I shall ride on my box,
That is like an ox,
Then go home with my box.

Alex Gore (9)
St Mary's Catholic Junior School, Newton-le-Willows

Why?

Why won't you tell me you love me
Before it is too late?
Why won't you tell me I'm needed
Before I walk through the gate?
Why won't you tell me there's something left
Worth saving for us to share?
Why won't you tell me I'm sometimes right
Or simply tell me that you still care?
Why if we've lost the love we once had
Why can't we try anew?
Why won't you let me prove to you
That I'm worth something too?

Emily Ablett (10)
St Mary's Catholic Junior School, Newton-le-Willows

The Magic Box

(Based on 'Magic Box' by Kit Wright)

I will put into the box . . .
A piece of happiness
A piece of sadness
A piece of the rainbow.

I will put into my box . . .
A piece of a twinkling star
A baby's first words
My old wishes.

I will put into my box . . .
A piece of the sun
A piece of the shining moon
A baby's first smile.

My box is made out of bright red rubies and bright silver crystals at the edges,
Pink fluff and some steal bars to protect it with some pictures of fishes on it.

I will put my box in the sea and let the mermaids and dolphins and fishes use it.

Holly Pegnam-Mason (9)
St Mary's Catholic Junior School, Newton-le-Willows

The Magic Box

(Based on 'Magic Box' by Kit Wright)

I will put in the box . . .
A picture of my mum, dad and Tas,
Some CD's, a little chocolate bar,
Hot chocolate, my Spanish dress and a sea wave.

I will put in the box . . .
Some clothes and a little TV,
The colour of the box is silver.

Demi-Lea Corr (8)
St Mary's Catholic Junior School, Newton-le-Willows

The Magic Box

(Based on 'Magic Box' by Kit Wright)

I will put in the box . . .
The scale of a fish
The tail of a monkey
The eye of a teacher.

I will put in the box . . .
The tooth of a friend
The head of a doll.

I will put in the box . . .
The dust of a fairy
The brain of Einstein,
A play by Shakespeare.

I will put in the box . . .
A bit of the world,
A bit of love,
The bud of a rose.

Devon Wright (9)
St Mary's Catholic Junior School, Newton-le-Willows

The Magic Box

(Based on 'Magic Box' by Kit Wright)

I will put in the box . . .

The first kick of a football
A baby's breath
My first holiday in Spain.

The box will be made from
Stars and owl feathers.

Bradley Woods (8)
St Mary's Catholic Junior School, Newton-le-Willows

The Magic Box

(Based on 'Magic Box' by Kit Wright)

I'll put into the box . . .

A newborn black Labrador in a red sports car,
A baby's first words
And a piece of the beautiful horizon.

I'll put into the box . . .

A monkey on a motorbike
A piece of happiness
And a piece of the fiery sun.

I'll put into the box . . .

A donkey singing in the shower
A hippo in a tutu
And a crocodile in a bathing suit.

My box is made from . . .
Sparkling red rubies, glistening crystals and diamonds.
I will go snowboarding in Switzerland with my box.

Hannah Morse (9)
St Mary's Catholic Junior School, Newton-le-Willows

The Magic Box

(Based on 'Magic Box' by Kit Wright)

I will put into the box . . .
A piece of blistering sun
The soul of my grandad
A piece of a shining star.

I will put into the box . . .
A baby's first kiss
A piece of happiness
A piece of the Atlantic Sea.

I will put into the box . . .
A heartbroken hamster
A piece of the moon
A Mary Jane doll.

My box is made of . . .
Pink snakeskin and red rubies.

What I will do with my box is
I will throw it into a volcano.

Emma Duxbury (9)
St Mary's Catholic Junior School, Newton-le-Willows

The Magic Box

(Based on 'Magic Box' by Kit Wright)

I will put into the box . . .
Fire from a dragon's mouth
Godzilla having a cup of tea
A monkey coming to school with me.

I will put into the box . . .
The raging wind of a tornado
A giant meteorite from outer space
And a piece of the fiery sun.

I will put into the box . . .
A stream of lava from a volcano
The shining emeralds of a stone
And the sound of thunder from a vicious storm.

My box is made of . . .
Shining emeralds
Surrounded by rubies
In a ring of sapphires.

I will
Give my box to Pikachu so he can guard it.

Jordan Wilcock (9)
St Mary's Catholic Junior School, Newton-le-Willows

The Magic Box

(Based on 'Magic Box' by Kit Wright)

I will put into the magic box . . .
An elephant who talks like a dog
A piece of happiness
A chocolate Christmas tree.

I will put into the magic box . . .
A piece of joy
A shiny expensive ruby
A piece of flying hair.

I will put into the magic box . . .
A see-through, glowing, powerful crystal
A broomstick made of white chocolate
A baby's first tooth.

My box is made from
Sparkling pink and purple material
With rubies, crystals, emeralds and a topaz.

I will make my box look nice and fashionable.

Natalie Forshaw (9)
St Mary's Catholic Junior School, Newton-le-Willows

The Magic Box

(Based on 'Magic Box' by Kit Wright)

I will put into the box . . .
The voice of an angel
A baby's first breath
And a piece of the sun.

I will put into the box . . .
A piece of the sky
Some lava from the very bottom of a volcano
And a baby's first cry.

I will put into the box . . .
A star from the night sky
An iceberg from the Atlantic Ocean and
A piece of the horizon.

I will put into the box . . .
A piece of water from the Mediterranean Sea
A lion from the jungle
And a piece of Saturn's ring.

My box is made from ice with stars for its hinges and a diamond lock.

I will sail on my box through the ocean.

Danielle Parker (8)
St Mary's Catholic Junior School, Newton-le-Willows

The Magic Box

(Based on 'Magic Box' by Kit Wright)

In my box it will have . . .
A piece of joy
And a piece of happiness
A fiery piece of the sun.

I will put in my box . . .
A piece of a colourful rainbow
Rich shining gold
And some hot melted lava.

I will put in my box . . .
Bright emeralds
Red rubies
And blue sapphires.

My box is made out of . . .
One large emerald
With rubies
And sapphires
With ice to protect it.

I will fly in the sky and play with birds
And pull faces at planes.

Ben Murphy (9)
St Mary's Catholic Junior School, Newton-le-Willows

The Magic Box

(Based on 'Magic Box' by Kit Wright)

I will put in my box . . .

A star from the night
And a torch shining bright
A picture of my family
A picture of my friend
But most of all my thoughts and memories
Will never end.

My box will be made out of . . .

Silver and gold
Some steel so old
Diamonds and jewels all so bright
They are so cool you know I am right!

My worst thoughts in my box are . . .

Falling out with my friends
And making friendships end
My family being lost
And that will really cost!

Rebecca Retford (9)
St Mary's Catholic Junior School, Newton-le-Willows

The Magic Box

(Based on 'Magic Box' by Kit Wright)

I will put in the box . . .

A picture of family,
A picture of friends,
A picture of pets and me,
So my memories never end.

I will put in the box . . .

A slice of the moon from the night
And a dream that makes me bright
And fun and games from all the fames,
That will help me sleep at night.

I will put in the box . . .

A holiday to remember,
With my family
And loads and loads more,
So I never let them free.

My box is so special,
My box is so small,
Just big enough to fit,
Everything short and tall.

Lauren Nolan (9)
St Mary's Catholic Junior School, Newton-le-Willows

The Highwayman

He steals from the rich
At the dark of night
Whoever he comes near
Gets a terrible *fright!*

He rides a black horse
Terrifying of course
Off he went
To rob the rich.

He went to the old inn door
To see his beloved beautiful Bess
With long black hair
But she was no more.

Laura Astley (9)
St Mary's Catholic Junior School, Newton-le-Willows

I Will Put In My Box

I will put in the box . . .
One of my locks
My dad's smelly old socks
And one of my mum's best frocks!

I will put in the box . . .
My sister's Saints top
A photo of my grandma
So my heart will stay locked!

I will put in the box . . .
My grandad's walking stick
My baby cousin's toy bricks
And Mathew's lolly for me to lick.

Lucy Boughey (8)
St Mary's Catholic Junior School, Newton-le-Willows

Animal Poem

A is for anteater who sniffs out ants
B is for budgie that tweets all day long
C is for cat that purrs all day long
D is for dog that barks a lot
E is for elephant that stamps his feet on the ground
F is for fish that swims around
G is for giraffe that is the tallest in the zoo
H is for hippo that is big and fat
 I is for imperial eagle that has wings 8 foot wide
J is for jaguar that is the second largest cat
K is for kangaroo that bounces up and down
L is for lizard that lives on the land
M is for macaw that eats nuts and berries
N is for night snake that lives in North America
O is for octopus that lives in the sea
P is for parrot that squawks a lot
Q is for quetzal that sits on a tree
R is for rattlesnake that is poisonous
S is for seal that swims through the water looking for food
T is for Tasmanian devil that is a carnivorous marsupial
U is for unicorn that is half human and half horse
V is for viper that can turn its fangs around
W is for wolves, which are meat eating and travel in packs
X is for x-ray fish that can be seen in x-ray when it's behind a plant
Y is for yak that can be wild or domestic
Z is for zebra that lives in Africa and has back and white stripes.

Gabby Hoinville (10)
St Mary's Catholic Junior School, Newton-le-Willows

The Magic Box

(Based on 'Magic Box' by Kit Wright)

I will put in my box . . .
My first football kit,
My favourite football,
My PSP and games.

I will put in my box . . .
The number off my motorbike,
A part of my first tooth
And a picture of my family.

I will put in my box . . .
My old pair of glasses,
My first pair of trainers,
A picture of my first bed.

I will put in my box . . .
My first piece of writing,
A picture of my dad's first car
And my jewellery.

Louis Pickering (9)
St Mary's Catholic Junior School, Newton-le-Willows

Quads

Quads can tow,
Quads can go,
Out there in the fields,
Quads are fun,
If I see them coming - I run,
I like quads,
I like quads,
Quads are fun.

Luachra Scott (7)
St Mary's Primary School, Enniskillen

Numbers

When I was 1, I saw my tum,
When I was 2, I said, 'Boo!'
When I was 3, I saw my knee,
When I was 4, I saw the floor,
When I was 5, I did a dive,
When I was 6, I added oil and mixed,
What will happen when I am seven?

Oran McCarney (6)
St Mary's Primary School, Enniskillen

Xbox

I played Medal of Honour,
I died a few times,
I got past the tank,
I got an Xbox 360,
I want to play it,
I got a phone.

Conor McCutcheon (6)
St Mary's Primary School, Enniskillen

Wind

The reason the Earth gets cold is because of me,
I fly around making people shiver,
When I'm happy I whistle on the windows of people's houses,
When someone leaves the door open,
I invite myself in and create a draught,
I love the sound of doors banging open or shut and people yelling,
I am invisible, I do what I want,
I am wind.

Lucy Seddon (10)
St Nicholas' CE Primary School, Liverpool

The Modern World

The modern world, though mysteries remain unsolved,
Is so refined and honed and polished.
Everything is so exact, yet I think that something's missing,
What happened to the good old days when nature reigned on high?

In the daytime our world is a hi-tech factory,
Everyone's working and rushing around in a hurry,
This working world is brilliant, yet I think that something's missing,
What happened to the good old days when nature reigned on high?

In the night-time our world is a prowling cat,
The street lamps are its glimmering eyes, never going out.
This night-time world is beautiful, yet I think that something's missing,
What happened to the good old days when nature reigned on high?

The modern world, though mysteries remain unsolved,
Is so refined and honed and polished.
Everything is so exact, yet I think that something's missing,
What happened to the good old days when nature reigned on high?

Alastair Cawdron (10)
St Nicholas' CE Primary School, Liverpool

Hallowe'en

Hallowe'en is coming,
People running,
Skeletons sucking,
Ghosts flying,
Children screaming,
Doors creaking,
Bats watching,
The bogeyman dancing,
Scarecrows scaring,
Pumpkin kings burning,
Devils gambling,
This is my Hallowe'en.

Patrick Clarke (11)
St Nicholas' CE Primary School, Liverpool

My Life

I was very, very small when my life began,
But now I'm tall, I'm almost a man,
It all started eleven years ago,
How long it will last I just don't know.

I gave my first smile at six weeks old,
By ten months I took my first step or so I've been told,
I was a joyful baby giggling and laughing,
Didn't know what at, but always smiling.

At two and a half, my family expanded,
My little brother had finally landed,
When he was born, he was very small,
But just like me, he's grown very tall.

The next big thing that happened to me,
Was starting school in Crosby,
The teachers were nice and very kind,
They have worked hard to develop my mind.

Now I am here, eleven years old,
I hope my life has not all been told.

Shaun Billows (11)
St Nicholas' CE Primary School, Liverpool

The Moon

The moon shone brightly,
On the cold, dusty ground,
There were no trees for miles,
Just flat bare land,
Nothing to the left, right, up or down,
Just the moon shining brightly,
On the cold, dusty ground.

Michael Bowyer (11)
St Nicholas' CE Primary School, Liverpool

Kill King Duncan

(Inspired by Macbeth)

Macbeth, my dear Macbeth,
Let's kill the king,
We will join in king and queen partnership,
Invite him to a party,
He thinks he is such a smartie.

Chop off his head,
That's what I said,
Chop, chop, chop,
Kill, kill, kill,
You will be king,
I will be queen.

We will run the kingdom,
Our reign will change the kingdom,
Kill King Duncan!

Jessica Wilson (10)
St Nicholas' CE Primary School, Liverpool

A Night Of Murder

This story starts upon a heath,
With three predictions made,
Thane of Cawdor and of Glamis,
The Scottish crown on his head laid.

His wife told him to murder Duncan,
For Macbeth's lady wanted power,
So Macbeth did the terrible deed,
In Duncan's sleeping hour.

Macbeth despaired of Duncan's death
And because the deed was done,
His lady cheered in happiness,
For the crown was won.

Ruth Cawdron (10)
St Nicholas' CE Primary School, Liverpool

About Lady Macbeth

(Inspired by Macbeth)

Lady Macbeth sat on her chair,
Wailing, fiddling with her hair,

She handed the daggers to Macbeth,
Who was about to put the king to his death,

She sat impatiently as the sin was done,
For she was not one for fear to run,

But she was grand and wealthy,
Yet still, not always healthy.

Brave Macbeth then came out,
And Lady Macbeth then gave a shout,

'You brave and noble man,' she lied,
People will bow down to you with pride.

For now he was to be king.

Heather Cunningham (10)
St Nicholas' CE Primary School, Liverpool

Valentine's Day

Valentine's Day, Valentine's Day
Is coming your way,
You better get started with the roses and cards
And all of your sweetheart's dreams that have come far
And don't forget them chocolates too,
Or your sweetheart will be disheartened.

So hurry up and don't delay!
Get all your sweetheart's gifts today,
Or if you don't then you shall have to wait,
Till next Valentine's Day
And then you shall have a date.

Abbey Jones (10)
St Nicholas' CE Primary School, Liverpool

Flowers

Daisies and foxgloves I have seen,
Red and brown leaves mainly green,
A rose, a symbol of true love,
A lily swaying in the air just like a dove,
A beautiful hyacinth glowing with power,
A sunflower growing higher than a tower,
A bluebell shivering far, far away
And there a snowdrop peacefully lay,
The villains are the ivy and holly,
But not the tulip standing there all jolly,
A poppy, the colour of blood,
A weed, oh no! They're no good,
A piece of food, for instance wheat,
All of the trees lined up in the street,
Freshly cut grass I like to smell,
I could tell the world, honestly,
I could tell.

Georgina Fox (11)
St Nicholas' CE Primary School, Liverpool

Dreamcatcher

Hanging on my bedroom wall,
Really a stunning sight,
A gigantic dreamcatcher plain white.

Turquoise beads and feathers too,
But I wonder of the magic within
And at night that horrible din.

Thrashing and clanging,
Unnatural some might say,
But it's only the beads keeping nightmares away.

Hanging on my bedroom wall,
Really a stunning sight,
A gigantic dreamcatcher of white.

Jessica Louise Fenlon (10)
St Nicholas' CE Primary School, Liverpool

Mirror

Every day I sit and stare,
People think I'm pretty bare,
I might be plain, but I'm polished,
Each day with love and care.

Every day I sit and wait
But at least I'm always straight,
Every day I'm tucked away,
I feel like I'm never going to stay.

I always feel like I'm never there,
Because no one even gives me a stare,
At least I get cleaned, I'm always gleaming,
Always bright like the stars tonight.

I like the pictures all around
But you can hear a sound from miles around.

Jamie Riley Hickey (11)
St Nicholas' CE Primary School, Liverpool

Seasons

In the summer it's very sunny,
When the bees go looking for honey.

In the winter it's very cold,
Wrap up as you'll be told.

In the spring the leaves will grow,
Right where we saw the snow.

In the autumn go get the rakes,
One rake is all it takes.

Sarah Leedham (11)
St Nicholas' CE Primary School, Liverpool

What Am I?

I can point to the left and can point to the right,
Sometimes I'm red and sometimes I can be white.

Occasionally I'm blue or yellow or even green,
I light up bright at night, so I can be seen.

Warn you, help you, I will be your guide,
You can always find me close to the roadside.

I'm triangular or square or maybe round,
I just stand there and don't make a sound.

I will always tell you the right way to go,
I could speed you up, or make you go slow.

Just look at me and I will tell you what to do,
What I say, is always true.

Oh no! Winding bends, so please take care,
Stray cattle ahead, you must beware!

Just follow my instructions to avoid a fine,
Oh what can I be?

A traffic road sign!

Joseph Duff (10)
St Nicholas' CE Primary School, Liverpool

Monday

I opened my eyes and what did I see?
A beautiful spread in front of me
A tail of dog, fried in a stew
One small cat's eye, floating in it too
Oh, what can I buy with my £1.23?
School dinner looks yummy to me.

Sarah Baden (10)
St Nicholas' CE Primary School, Liverpool

An Only Child (I Wish!)

My life started quite good at first,
My mum and dad loved me,
Until I burst,
I cried and cried as they could see,
They loved me for me,
Until I turned 3,
My sister was born,
One day my grandad, David,
Was mowing his lawn,
Then I turned older and taller,
But Megan got to 2,
A boy was born, Adam,
He was always a bad baby,
He ripped wallpaper
And would never stop,
Until a dummy had been given to him
And the screaming and shouting all went pop
And then he also got given a blue blanket,
Then I turned 8,
Megan got to 5
And Adam was 3
And it was time to throw Adam's dummy away,
Here we are in 2006,
I am 10 and in Year 6,
Megan is 7 and in Year 3
Adam is 5 and in Reception
And we are all happy to be.

Melissa Wilding (10)
St Nicholas' CE Primary School, Liverpool

The Car Boot Sale

Once I went to the car boot sale,
Run by three witches,
They were offering very expensive pictures,
Did they rob them, or break free from jail?

In the car boot sale there was,
Cups of human blood,
A sandwich made out of mud,
The most disgusting that I saw,
Was frog toasties made from the poor.

Suddenly, a clap of thunder,
It started to make me wonder,
Why the witches had gone so soon,
Why hadn't they left at noon?

All around me, no escape,
Because the witches had gone off with their cape,
Collapsed bodies surrounded me,
I wouldn't be home for tea.

My mum was wondering where I was.
A whimper, a squeal,
That is what I hear every time my mum has a meal,
Because shortly after the thunderstorm,
I was taken away by those witches,
Now I'm counting up how many days I have to live.

Elizabeth Wood (11)
St Nicholas' CE Primary School, Liverpool

SpongeBob SquarePants

There once was a sponge called SpongeBob,
Who lived in the deep blue sea,
With friends called Patrick and Sandy,
Who were as close as friends could be.

They have many adventures in the ocean,
With challenges stretching far and wide,
Sometimes he will be in danger,
But a friend's always by his side.

He works at the Krusty Krab restaurant,
With spatula, grill and fries,
He makes the perfect patty
And that you can't deny.

So if you're ever swimming
And meet this friend of mine,
Be sure to go to his pineapple,
He'll welcome you anytime.

Peter Jones (11)
St Nicholas' CE Primary School, Liverpool

Friendship

Friendship will never end,
Because you will always have a best friend,
Always there when you're alone,
In school or on the phone,
Playing all day in the sun,
Having lots and lots of fun,
This friendship will never end,
Because you will always be my best friend.

Katie Jewell (11)
St Teresa's Junior School, Liverpool

Everton

With great players like Cahill and Arteta,
Everton seem to be getting better and better.

On match day when all the fans are excited,
David Moyes prepares for Everton Vs Man United.

Walking into the stadium to watch their team play,
James Beattie prepares for the game of the day.

It's kick off and before you could even blink,
Kevin Kilbane scores and United minds sink.

It's half-time, we're leading one goal to nil,
Then comes out the players starting with Tim Cahill.

Then all of a sudden, Beattie attacks with the ball,
He shoots, he scores, and the opposition nearly starts a brawl.

At the end we win the game
And the fans shout every player's name.

Mark Seddon (10)
St Teresa's Junior School, Liverpool

Liverpool

L is for the lively team
I is for in and out of Europe in 90 minutes (Everton)
V is for victory
E is for Everton who aren't as good
R is for red which we play in
P is for playing the beautiful game
O is for Owen who was a great player
O is for owning our great club
L is for Liverpool, the best team in the Premiership.

Nyle Dennis (11)
St Teresa's Junior School, Liverpool

What Is Blue?

The sea is blue,
It's there for me and you.
What else is blue? The sky,
Always there up high.
Blue is a police car,
Still loud from so far.

Pond, pool, boat, scarf or cap,
Blue is to fill in the gap.

Blue is cold and shakes in winter,
That's even worse than getting a splinter,
Until it's too much to stand
And you end up with chocolate in hand,
Now I'm going to wrap up,
With a hot chocolate cup,
So remember that blue . . . is blue!

James Deegan (10)
St Teresa's Junior School, Liverpool

Happiness

H is for happiness which grows on our faces
A is for anyone that will put a smile on our face
P is for people who make everyone smile
P is for people who will be there for us all the time
 I is for independent people who know that we are right
N is for never, never-ending happiness
E is for everywhere happiness is
S is for snow, which makes us smile with the glow
S is for so you know that - *happiness is here*!

Geraldine Brown (10)
St Teresa's Junior School, Liverpool

What Am I . . . ?

I am danger and hard to spot,
I am like a king or queen,
I am small or maybe big,
I am feared because . . .
I can kill,
What am I?

Sean Kelly (10)
St Teresa's Junior School, Liverpool

Me Compared To Everton

A lot of people say Tim Cahill is the best,
But you haven't see me bring it down on my chest,
Some people say Duncan Ferguson is the Hulk!
But you don't want to see him when I sulk!
When David Moyes is shouting on the line,
His voice is nothing compared to mine,
When they go home in their big flashy cars,
I have to walk back to ours
And when they get a cook in their house,
I go back home to find Mum's home-made scouse.

Ellie Moss
St Teresa's Junior School, Liverpool

Summer

S is for a hot sun
U is for no umbrella
M is for me having fun
M is for my cousins joining in
E is for everyone having ice cream
R is for relaxing in the sun.

Lauren Broomfield (10)
St Teresa's Junior School, Liverpool

Me And My Friends

Me and my friends have so much fun,
We are like glitter shining in the sun.

When I need them they are there,
This just shows that they care.

My best friend is, well I don't know,
I hope our friendship will never go.

We are all best friends forever,
We'll never split up, no not ever.

I go to their parties and to their house,
But when I'm there I'm as quiet as a mouse.

I am happy to be their friend,
Look at the valuable time we spend.

My friends and I do a lot of talking,
Let alone all the walking.

So if you are a real friend,
Make sure your friendship never ends.

Bethan Williams (11)
St Teresa's Junior School, Liverpool

The Very Best Of Friends!

We talk in literacy,
We talk in maths
And most likely during our SATs,
We talk on the playground
And on the way home,
Then at the gate
And then on the phone,
My mum wishes our talking would end,
But what else do you do with your very
Best friend?

Daniella Cody (11)
St Teresa's Junior School, Liverpool

Vandalism Is Sly

Bus smasher,
Car crasher,
Write on walls,
Prank phone calls,
Anti-social behaviour,
Could be major,
Might be fires,
Just because you're the liars,
People die, so this is sly,
Go to jail,
Then you bail,
Robbing stuff,
Being rough,
Don't do this you'll end up in danger,
Could end up hurting a stranger.

Sophie O'Hare (10)
St Teresa's Junior School, Liverpool

My Mum's Love For Me!

Some people think that Gerrard's great
And yes he may be,
But no one beats my mum,
When it comes to loving me,
She tucks me in at night-time and kisses me goodnight
And then she says up close to me,
'Night-night, don't let the bed bugs bite!'

Peggy May Brown (11)
St Teresa's Junior School, Liverpool

Nature Is Beautiful

The flowers sway pink and blue
Out in the colourful bay
I heard the bird singing out loud
It was so beautiful I thought
It was from the cloud.

Sarah Kilbride (10)
St Teresa's Junior School, Liverpool

The Tiger - Haiku

The tiger is black
It stares at you with green eyes
I was very scared.

Abbie Coaley (9)
St Teresa's Primary School, St Helens

What Is Fantasy?

Angels and fairies
With beautiful wings
Butterflies and daisies
And sweet girlish things!

What is fantasy?

Animals and bugs
Looking at me
In the toadstool
Café having a cup of tea!

Charis Wadsworth (10)
St Teresa's Primary School, St Helens

In The Jungle

Crawling in the jungle
Crawling in the grass
Lurking for some supper
As the tiger prowls.

Swinging in the jungle
Swinging from tree to tree
Swinging for bananas
Yes! It's the monkey too!

Trumpeting, trumpeting
Squirting water
Cleaning off, cooling down
Elephants walk all around.

Tweet, tweet,
Peck, peck,
Squawk, squawk,
Parrots are annoying!

Slither, slither
Hiss, hiss
Snakes slither all around us!

Ashleigh Lee (10)
St Teresa's Primary School, St Helens

Summer Days

S ummer is great
U nder the sun children like to play
M ums go crazy about not getting burnt
M adness is allowed
E veryone eating ice cream
R abbits are all around me.

Tom Fairclough (9)
St Teresa's Primary School, St Helens

Butterflies

B utterflies are colourful, they are such a lovely sight,
U nder the branch they go when it rains, they suffer from snow
   so they play little games,
T hey fly around flowers and round they go, they have pretty colours,
   we love them so,
T rees sway in the breeze and sometimes the butterflies freeze,
E mma is my name and I like butterflies, they flutter in the sky,
R unning around a little boy tries to catch a little butterfly,
F lying round, up and down the little butterfly soon would be found,
L ying still in my bed, I woke up and banged my head but still
   the butterfly was there,
Y ou and me love them so, I like to watch them flow.

Emma O'Hanlon (9)
St Teresa's Primary School, St Helens

On The Beach!

On the beach the sea is clear,
My dad's sunbathing with a glass of beer!

The ships are miles out at sea,
We can have fun together you and me!

Today it's hot so put your suncream on,
You don't want to get burnt by the sun!

Then we can build sandcastles,
After that we can collect some fossils!

Today's been great but I have to go now,
There are so many things I've found out, wow!

Keeley Potter (9)
St Teresa's Primary School, St Helens

In The Jungle

In the jungle
Mighty lions roar
Pythons sliding through the trees
I don't dare open my door.

In the desert
Camels plod along
Walking for miles and miles
All day long.

In the ocean
A shark swims by
Eating tons of fishes
He stares with his big eyes.

In the sky
Eagles swoop and soar
Hunting mice and rabbits
On the rocky floor.

George Dalton (10)
St Teresa's Primary School, St Helens

Liverpool

L iverpool is the best
I ncluding Barcelona
V illa is a team I hate
E verton are quite good
R onaldinho is the best at skill
P ires is on Arsenal
O lé he might go
O lé Gerrard will go
L iverpool will score the *goal!*

Declan Navin (9)
St Teresa's Primary School, St Helens

No School

School, school
No people in school
Teachers at home eating corned beef
What a day.

School, school
Everyone likes school
Kids happy, teachers mad
What a day.

School, school
I love school,
Girls reading, boys writing
What a day, I mean *what a day!*

Joe Coates (10)
St Teresa's Primary School, St Helens

Sea Creatures

Dolphins jumping all around
Fishes swimming towards the ground
Squeaking noises, hear the sound.

Fish love to swim and feed,
Dolphins jumping, they feel the breeze.

Jellyfish like to wobble along,
Turtles singing a beautiful song.

Sharks biting with their sharp teeth
Jellyfish stinging with their burning feet.

Rachel Ratcliffe (10)
St Teresa's Primary School, St Helens

Liverpool

L iverpool are the best
I love Liverpool
V ery important that they win the cup
E very time they win, I celebrate
R obbie Fowler is the best
P ongolle is good
O h we won the cup
O h what a *goal!*
L *iverpool are champs!*

Jack Woodward (9)
St Teresa's Primary School, St Helens

Running In The Jungle

Running in the jungle, hear the lions roar
Monkeys swinging in the trees
See the birds soar.

Rhinos, tigers and crocodiles too
Keep running on or they will be after you!

Down by the sea, animals play
On this hot summer day.

Running in the jungle!

Jade Morrissey (10)
St Teresa's Primary School, St Helens

Everton

E verton is da best
V illa is a team I hate
E verton, it's a *goal!*
R ight corner, it's a *goal!*
T oday is Everton day
O h yeah
N o one gets away without a fight!

Aaron Ellison
St Teresa's Primary School, St Helens

Dragon's Diary

Monday:
Today I went to the dentist,
He must have thought me malicious,
My teeth were not quite to his taste,
But I thought that *he* was delicious!

Tuesday:
I went to the gym today,
I think I make people afraid,
When I stepped onto the running machine,
They ran like I'd thrown a grenade!

Wednesday:
Today I visited Mummy,
She wanted to go to the zoo,
Sadly we got thrown out,
She got hungry and ate a gnu!

Thursday:
I went shopping at Tesco today,
The trolley didn't seem to like me,
I tried to turn left, but *it* turned right,
I bet people thought I was silly!

Friday:
I went to Ripperclaw's cave today,
BBQs are his talent,
Especially when it's cow or sheep,
Or even a knight so gallant!

Daisy Easton (9)
Saltergate Junior School, Harrogate

Would You Cook?

Would you cook a horse in sauce?
Would you cook a duck with a recipe book?
Would you cook a frog from a bog?
Would you cook a cat with a bat?
Would you cook a squid in the river Nidd?

Joshua James Watson (8)
Saltergate Junior School, Harrogate

Blue

Blue is the colour of the sky,
Blue is the colour when you say bye,
Blue is the colour of a football shirt,
Blue is the colour of when you're alert.

That is blue!

Andrew Mellor (8)
Saltergate Junior School, Harrogate

The Teacher And The Lobster

Mr Jones, the teacher, went to the beach,
A fine lobster he could see,
He asked the lobster, 'Would you care to come and
Help me teach?'

He brought the lobster home,
Looking at the lobster he was ready for some food,
He picked up the lobster, bright red and nude,
'Are you going to eat me?' cried the lobster,
'No, no, of course not,' he imagined it fried,
'Have a hot bath, my dear friend,' he said to the creature,
Then sadly the lobster was eaten by the teacher.

Peter Jones (8)
Saltergate Junior School, Harrogate

Black

Black is as black as a witch's cat,
Black is the colour of a witch's hat.

Black is as black as a monster's caves,
Black is the colour when a monster shaves.

Black is as black as shovelled coal,
Black is the colour of a deep, dark hole.

Rachel Garner (8)
Saltergate Junior School, Harrogate

Lee And The Ogre

Poor little Lee was only four,
When he met an ogre by the door.
'Hello Lee, my little friend,
Now your life must come to an end!'

Before Lee knew it, he'd grabbed his head,
'In ten minutes you will be dead!'
Suddenly, he'd began to shoot up to the sky!
Lee thought it was way too high.

'Wait a minute ogre, how can you fly?'
'It doesn't matter, you will soon die!'
And with that, he dropped poor Lee . . .
Into the huge and angry sea!

. . . *Splash!*
Lee could smell bangers and mash!
Lee opened his eyes and saw his red and blue bed,
'I'll forget my memories from last night in my head!'

Hopefully, last night was not true
And suddenly he wanted the loo,
This boy was called Lee Mackoger,
He opened the bedroom door and saw the ogre!

The ogre roared and swallowed him whole,
The usual for an ogre was a fat round mole,
The ogre burped, it was a lovely tea,
Sadly that was the end of poor little Lee!

Sam Longbottom-Smith (11)
Saltergate Junior School, Harrogate

Love Is

Love is as sweet as sugar,
Love is the sound of a harp,
Love is a red heart,
Love is the feel of a baby,
Love is the smell of perfume.

Megan Childs (8)
Saltergate Junior School, Harrogate

The Child And The Strawberries

The child went to the strawberry tree,
To the strawberry tree she said,
'Would you like to come to my house for tea?
Then go to my nice warm bed?'
The head strawberry thought, then said,
'Of course we'll come if you give us some tea
And a nice warm bed.'
So off to her house they went.
When they got to her kitchen
The strawberries got a horrible scent,
For they'd seen the cream on the table,
This made the strawberries feel unstable,
So the child started making tea,
When she started making it,
She started to see,
That the strawberries went one by one,
Until they'd all gone.

Katherine Weaver (8)
Saltergate Junior School, Harrogate

Broccoli

Bobby ate bobble broccoli all the time,
When he went to ask his mum,
'What's for tea?'
His mum always said, 'Broccoli, hee, hee.'
But when he went to play
He felt a twitch on his head,
So he went to look in the mirror,
Then he screamed
And ran away,
His head had turned green,
He could not stop the scream.

Chloe Broom (8)
Saltergate Junior School, Harrogate

Friendship

Friendship is as sweet as honey,
Friendship is being together,
Friendship is friends forever,
Friendship is the smell of roses,
Friendship looks like a mother smiling,
Friendship sounds of sweet songs
Coming from the sky.

Ella Benson (9)
Saltergate Junior School, Harrogate

The Kid And The Blueberry

The kid went to a blueberry tree,
The blueberry said, 'Don't eat me.'
'I know you're so juicy and up above,' the kid said,
'Blueberries I love.'
'I'm up high above your head
But if you eat me, I'll be dead.'
The kid said, 'I know you'll die,
Then your friends will weep and cry.'

Niamh Johnson (8)
Saltergate Junior School, Harrogate

Yellow

Yellow is the colour of the golden sun,
Yellow is the smell of a vanilla bun,
Yellow is the skin of a ripe banana,
Yellow looks like a smiling flower,
Yellow rolls like a bouncy ball,
Yellow slides on the slippery floor,
Yellow is the colour of a sailor's T-shirt,
Yellow is as flat as a piece of paper.

Marina Godin (8)
Saltergate Junior School, Harrogate

Yellow

Yellow is the colour of bright fireworks,
Yellow is the smell of fruity lemon,
It sparkles everywhere,
Yellow is the colour of joy,
When I see yellow I feel happy,
Yellow is the colour of a warm fire burning.

Bethany Grace (8)
Saltergate Junior School, Harrogate

Boredom

Boredom is the teacher, yapping on about curtains
and the government all day long,
Boredom is endless 'Countdown' on TV,
Boredom is reading 'Cardboard Lovers' magazine,
Boredom is also uncle's cheese factory holiday pics and hours of
holiday videos,
Boredom also includes watching paint dry all day,
But the most boring of all,
Boredom is writing about boredom.

Sam Leverton (9)
Saltergate Junior School, Harrogate

Irritation

Irritation feels horrible and mouldy,
It smells like mushy peas,
It looks like a donkey eating with its mouth open,
It tastes like bogies,
It sounds like a bad trumpet player.

Sean Lawes (8)
Saltergate Junior School, Harrogate

Irritation!

Irritation feels like a big sledgehammer banging on your fragile head,
It tastes like a big snotty bogey with a boy attached,
It smells like burnt toast,
Just come out the toaster,
Irritation is my brother dressing up as Eminem
And trying to rap like him.

Christian Mortimer (9)
Saltergate Junior School, Harrogate

Chips

Chips, chips, glorious chips,
Chips, chips, send me to Heaven,
Chips, chips, my favourite song,
Chips, chips, smooth and soft,
Chips, chips, fish and chips,
Chips for dinner, lunch and tea,
Chips in the bathtub,
Chips for free,
Chips in the school room,
Chips for me.

Thomas Hemingway (8)
Saltergate Junior School, Harrogate

Worry

The colour of worry is pitch-black,
The sound is floorboards creaking below you,
It feels like the cold, hard, concrete walls
And all you can see is the locked up doors.

Matthew Younger (8)
Saltergate Junior School, Harrogate

Fear

Fear feels like a spider crawling down your back,
Fear smells like a greasy armpit,
Fear sounds like a strangled cat,
Fear tastes like a furry lump of cat hair,
Fear looks like mouldy feet sticking out of a coffin.

Kieran Borchard (9)
Saltergate Junior School, Harrogate

Boringness

Boringness is
Dull rainy days when the wind is blowing,
Going to Asda and wishing your mum would go and pay,
Going to school,
Having to stay in and watch a game of pool,
Boringness is
Shopping for hours for clothes,
A one hour meeting about toes,
It's all boring!

Rebecca Griffith (9)
Saltergate Junior School, Harrogate

Silliness

Silliness smells like a wibbly jelly wobbling about,
Silliness tastes like a gooey snake stuck to your teeth,
Silliness feels like someone stepping in really smelly cow poo,
Silliness looks like a boy falling in a wet muddy puddle,
Silliness sounds like a cow singing karoke in the town centre.

Megan Kenyon (9)
Saltergate Junior School, Harrogate

The Haunted Doll

I looked at its evil angry eyes,
Because of that, I told loads of lies,
I remembered the chainsaw and the blood,
The doll had killed then, threw up its hood.
That night it wasn't all that it seemed,
The doll's eyes flickered then I screamed,
Sam was my best friend, better than a mate,
His best hobby was to roller-skate,
The doll threw an axe, which went right through,
Nobody knows how much it can do.
I screeched in mercy and in pain,
I cried in anger and in vain.
Almost like my deceased, massacred friend,
The terror jumped upon my back,
Then tied me up inside its sack,
Now I knew it, I was truly dead,
The horror cackled inside its head,
I won't forget the haunted doll!

Ben Longbottom-Smith (11)
Saltergate Junior School, Harrogate

Silliness

It smells like a fizzy jelly snake up your nose,
It tastes like a baby eating an alarm clock,
It looks like a sheep shopping and a donkey in Asda,
It feels like Jesus writing on his cross,
It sounds like a banana screaming
And that's what I feel like when I'm silly.

James Bennison (9)
Saltergate Junior School, Harrogate

The Man In The Sun And The Man In The Moon

You may know of the man in the moon
But do you know that morning and noon
The man in the sun awakes?

He stirs the sleepy world with great rays of light
More glowing than a diamond bright
But not a sound he makes.

No matter the mood of the new day
He will shine on anyway
Until he goes to sleep.

The man in the moon called out to the stars
They all came out from afar
And into the sky they did leap.

Moon grinned and laughed, with glee
Like a glittering coin in a huge black sea
Filling the sun with anger.

'How dare you steal my stage!'
Screeched the sun with rage
'It is I that shines stronger.'

'Oh Sun, silly Sun you know you agree
That the best is surely me
Glowing is a talent of mine.'

'I'm the brightest!'
They both shouted
At exactly the same time.

Mahala Woodhouse (10)
Saltergate Junior School, Harrogate

Silliness

The silliest thing is a cat driving a car
Or a granny being a pop star,
What about a person talking to their feet,
It's just strange for a baby to tap to the beat,
It's being silly for an ant to play football,
Or a mouse swimming in a waterfall.
You would never see a crumb being shot at,
Silly is a person being electrocuted.

Even an ant having a four metre baby
And it is so silly for an adult to watch Noddy,
It's so silly for a monkey to go to Marks & Spencer
And a person to go and pet her,
But the first prize goes to a fish eating a cat
Or a human eating a cowpat!

Connor McAlister-Payne (9)
Saltergate Junior School, Harrogate

Wickedness

It looks like someone poking a cat's eye out,
It feels like needles stabbed into your hand,
It smells like burning flesh,
It sounds like you've made a million babies cry,
It tastes like fireworks in your mouth.

Jonathan Korcu (9)
Saltergate Junior School, Harrogate

Confusion

Confusion is a dizzy swirl,
Confusion is a curly curl,
Dizziness feels like being knocked out,
Confusion may also make you shout,
Confusion is a monkey's head gone completely wrong,
Confusion also makes the place pong!
The wheels in your head have broken down,
You walk around like a moron around the town,
You make your smoothies terribly wrong,
When you sing it's not a song,
You feel so dizzy, I can tell
Now you, I really want to sell!

Nicole Leaver (9)
Saltergate Junior School, Harrogate

Mrs McFlea

Mrs McFlea who lives in North Wales
Ate cold pizza whilst standing on scales,
She thought that the diet would slim her, it failed!
Pizza for breakfast, pizza for tea,
'I love pizza' said Mrs McFlea.

Mrs McFlea will eat pizza forever
And if she does, there'll be no plan to stop her,
She'll turn into a king-sized margarita
And all the fat pigeons would land to eat her.

Kassie Morris (8)
Saltergate Junior School, Harrogate

Let's Communicate!

Why not listen to a song?
You can even sing along.

Text a message to your sister,
Let her know that you have missed her.

Post a *Get Well* card to Auntie Jill,
Did you know that she's been quite ill?

Try to learn some semaphore,
Before you think of leaving shore!

Remember to phone your mum
Let her know you're having fun.

Send an email to all the crew,
I'm sure they'd love to hear from you!

Please turn on the radio,
Will it rain or will it snow?

Why not watch some TV
Sit down with all the family.

Send an invitation to Marty
Ask him to come and join the party!

Write a postcard to Auntie Sue,
She might even write back to you.

And don't forget to post Grandma's letter,
Hope that she is feeling better.

When there's nothing left to hear or say,
Smile, and begin again the following day!

Class BW (9/10)
Seamer & Irton CP School, Scarborough

The Story Of Bob Who Would Not Sleep

Bob was a sleepy lad;
Dark circles under his eyes he had
And everybody saw him snore,
As he sleepwalked into the door,
Sleepy Bob whinges and groans,
Like a little baby moans.
Bob told his mum he could not sleep
And frightened Mum and made her leap.
He would not do as he was told
And his dark circles became very bold.

But one day - one cold winter's day,
He screamed out - 'I've had enough,
I am really beginning to feel rough.'

Next day his mother said,
'You must go to bed,
Naughty Bob you bad boy;
If you don't go to sleep I'll dispose of your best toy.'
'I'm sorry,' Bob said, 'I can't get to sleep,
Because of the cars going beep, beep, beep.'

The third day comes: he still couldn't sleep
And in a maths lesson he fell in a heap.
The class teacher angrily said:
'You silly boy you'd better go home and get to bed.'
He went to the swimming pool
And fell in so people thought he was a fool.

The fourth day comes: Bob couldn't be found,
His dad said, 'Please get to bed, I'll give you a pound.'
Bob finally came home with his sleepy head,
And Dad screamed out, 'Get to bed!'
Bob eventually went to bed
And with his snoring, gave everyone a sore head.

Class PC (8/9)
Seamer & Irton CP School, Scarborough

The Circle Of Time

Winter's grasp, smothering the green Earth
Transforming into shiny diamonds and ice
Enveloping all in its blanket of glittery mist
Freezing life, like a statue in its grinding path.

Spring's reach, uncovering winter's startling shock
Appetising wilderness, new hopeful beginnings
Developing buds, blossom and bees searching
Rising, burning sun, alarming yet glorious.

Summer's entrance, melting shoreline strolls
Sounds of laughter, playing through the air
Feelings of breaths of happiness
Meeting the golden scorching sun.

Autumn's breeze, colours crunching underfoot
Smoke drifting in smooth, unpredictable waves
Bursting, swirling, spirals in the sky
A complete seasonal *circle of time*.

Class LC (10/11)
Seamer & Irton CP School, Scarborough

Food! Food!

Food, food, glorious food, nothing quite like it when you're in a mood!
Cherry, cherry, glorious cherry, a wonderful fruit, a wonderful berry!
Turkey, turkey, glorious turkey, when you get tired,
                              it makes you feel perky!
Cake, cake, glorious cake, ooh . . . I've got a tummy ache!

Jessica Edwards (9)
Settle Primary School, Settle

Floss

Floss has a black wet nose,
Floss likes to lick our toes.

Floss doesn't like cats,
Floss likes tickles and pats.

Floss always sits at the gate,
Floss is my best mate.

Danielle Milner (10)
Settle Primary School, Settle

My Mum And My Dad!

My dad does the getting up early,
My mum takes us to school,
My mum works in the house,
My dad delivers the post,
Then my mum does the cooking
And my dad does the washing,
My mum takes us to bed,
My dad sometimes too,
Then my mum and dad go downstairs
And me and my sister sleep.

Emma Louise Leeming (9)
Settle Primary School, Settle

Temperature

As chilly as the winter's breeze passing by,
As hot as the sweating classroom on a summer's day,
As boiling as an overheating car,
As cold as my hands walking to school on a winter's day.

Grace McSharry (8)
Settle Primary School, Settle

Within

Within a book is paper,
Within the paper is wood,
Within the wood burns a fire,
Within the felt melts a stone,
Within the stone is lava,
Within the lava is a ring,
Within the ring is love,
Within the love is a heart,
Within the heart is a sea,
Within the sea reflects the sky,
Within the sky is the sun,
Within the sun is a bird,
Within the bird is a flow of song,
Within song is a world of joy
And in joy is you.

Rosie Ralph (9)
Settle Primary School, Settle

Going To Get Meat!

I'm riding down the street,
Going to get some meat,
Fall off my seat,
On my feet.

I'm walking down the street,
Got my meat,
Sit down on a seat,
Oh no! I squashed my meat.

I'm running down the street,
Without my meat,
See some people sitting down on a seat,
Oh no! Mum's going to stamp on my feet.

Joe Bennison (9)
Settle Primary School, Settle

It Was Long Ago

I'll tell you shall I? Something I remember,
Something that still means a great deal to me,
It was long ago.

A lit up sitting room in winter I remember,
A Santa hat and a scarf and some knitting needles you know.

In the sitting room, a Santa outfit I remember,
With white and red on it,
Me staring.

I walked over the beige carpet
And I remember Santa looking at me,
It was long ago.

How it felt to be three and Nana called out,
'Merry Christmas!'
And I went to sit on her knee.

That is the farthest thing I can remember,
It won't mean much to you,
It does to me,
Then I grew older you see.

Molly Riley (8)
Settle Primary School, Settle

My Friend

My friend is bigger than me,
As anyone can see.

If I grow bigger than her,
Everyone will see,
That I'm bigger than her,
She's not bigger than me.

Laura Whorton (9)
Settle Primary School, Settle

The Warlords

The warrior stands,
His battle armour gleaming a bright green,
His chaingun bursting with flames,
With bullets popping out of the barrel,
Shining in the sun,
But we never see his face,
He is the warlord.

While aliens leap,
With blades reflecting in moonlight,
Green skin, gold tattoos, a warlord's mask,
White fangs and glowing red eyes,
His poisonous Razik flashing green,
These are the enemy,
The very threat to the human race.

Jacob Dryden (9)
Settle Primary School, Settle

Rainbow

Rainbow, rainbow, you're colourful and amazing,
All different shapes and sizes,
Your colours are amazing but what are they?

First red like an apple,
Then orange like a tiger,
Then yellow from the sun,
Then green as the grass,
Then blue like the sea,
Then indigo like a flower,
Finally violet like a sweet pea.

I just can't wait
Till I get the gold.

Bethany Kate Fell
Settle Primary School, Settle

There Was A Young Lady From Brazil

There was a young lady from Brazil,
Who decided to carve with a chisel,
She cut herself badly
And bandaged it gladly
And lived did the lady of Brazil.

Alex Peter Tarbox (9)
Settle Primary School, Settle

Temperature

As lukewarm as the microwave being heated up,
As chilly as a shady place where the trees hang over you,
As boiling as the sun beating down on you,
As cold as a penguin shivering in the Antarctic,
As freezing as a little boy shivering in the playground.

George Gowland (8)
Settle Primary School, Settle

Temperature

As cold as snow, just like slush in a drink,
As boiling as fire when it's white outside,
As freezing as a freezer cooling lollies,
Warm as the classroom at midday.

Elliott Lee (8)
Settle Primary School, Settle

Temperature

As tepid as the shower when I get in,
As cold as the freezer when you touch it,
As boiling as an oven getting ready to start.

Hugh Francmanis (8)
Settle Primary School, Settle

Temperature

As freezing as oven chips sitting in my freezer,
As chilly as the shower when the heater is broken,
As boiling as my fire warming everyone up,
As hot as a cup of tea when my dad is drinking it.

Jack Horsfall (8)
Settle Primary School, Settle

Temperature

As cold as my house with the central heating off,
As freezing as myself walking home from school,
As hot as my fire when I sit in front of it.

Steven Capstick (8)
Settle Primary School, Settle

Temperature

As boiling as an oven in the evening cooking the tea,
As cold as a fridge that stores all the food,
As lukewarm as a flower in the field when the sun is shining on it,
As chilly as the snow when it falls on you,
As freezing as a freezer when you open it up,
As tepid as a bulb when it's starting to run out.

Cameron Brook (7)
Settle Primary School, Settle

Temperature

As boiling as an oven crackling in the steamy kitchen,
As chilly as a man stood still in the middle of winter,
As cold as the deep blue sea next to the sunny island,
As hot as a microwave going round and round in the kitchen,
As freezing as water turning into cubes of ice.

Shannon Louise Shortreed (8)
Settle Primary School, Settle

It Was Long Ago

I'll tell you shall I? Something I remember,
Something that still means a great deal to me,
It was long ago.

A house and a dog you know,
Inside the house, a dog I remember,
Black and white, barking in a seat,
Eating a bone with the sharpest teeth.

He seemed to be the youngest thing I can remember,
But then perhaps I was not more than four,
It was long ago.

I fell off the chair and I remember,
How my mum looked at me
And seemed to know.

That is the farthest thing I can remember,
It won't mean much to you but it does to me,
Then I grew up you see.

Louis Connor Gill (8)
Settle Primary School, Settle

Temperature Poem

As hot as the burning hot oven I bake my cakes in,
As freezing as the icicles on my cold shed,
As tepid as the radiators on a warm temperature,
As chilly as the cold wintry wind, outside my house,
As boiling as the kettle steaming out smoke,
As lukewarm as the stretch in my body,
As cold as the wind on a windy cold day.

Holly Mae Thornton (8)
Settle Primary School, Settle

It Was Long Ago

I'll tell you shall I? Something
That still means a great deal to me,
It was long ago.

A pink and gold night in
The spring I remember,
A little blue tractor and a toy bear
That was mine you know.

Behind the tractor was a man you know
He looked at me and winked.

He seemed the oldest thing I can remember
But perhaps I was not more than three,
It was long ago.

That is the farthest thing I can remember,
It won't mean much to you, it does to me
Then I grew older you see.

Sam Laycock (8)
Settle Primary School, Settle

Temperature

As freezing as a padlock on a cold frosty road,
As lukewarm as the wind blowing in my hair,
As hot as a cake coming out the oven,
As chilly as the wind hitting my ear,
As boiling as the sun on a hot summer's day,
As cold as a bird's wings next to my face,
As tepid as a breeze shooting on the windowpane.

Kieran Illingworth (8)
Settle Primary School, Settle

Temperature Poem

As boiling as the sun reflecting off the floor,
As hot as the teacher when a pupil has gone mad,
As freezing as the snowman standing outside my house,
As tepid as a winter leaf from a tree.

Rowan Ashley Carpenter (8)
Settle Primary School, Settle

Snowflakes

Snowflakes
Flutter
Silently to
The ground.

Like a carpet of snow
Until the children
Come out to play

And then it
Is ruined and
Fades away.

Lauren Smith (9)
Settle Primary School, Settle

Temperature Poem

As freezing as a freezer, waiting to be opened.
As lukewarm as a boiled egg, being put out on the plate.
As boiling as the sun, sizzling in the sky.
As tepid as a chicken, just being born.

Robert Adam Scaife (7)
Settle Primary School, Settle

Temperature Poem

As boiling as a twinkly sun,
As cold as a sparkly sea,
As tepid as my lovely bubblebath,
As lukewarm as my milk on my cereal,
As hot as a dark sauna,
As freezing as my icy freezer.

Erin Scarlet Cokell (7)
Settle Primary School, Settle

Temperature Poem

As freezing as snow when you fall on the ground,
As chilly as an ice cream melting in the sun,
As lukewarm as a radiator leaking dreadfully,
As boiling as an oven burning all the food,
As cold as a water fountain when you fall in,
As tepid as cold and warm water in the bath,
As hot as a fire crackling loudly.

Tara McManus (8)
Settle Primary School, Settle

Temperature Poem

As cold as a lollipop,
Waiting to be eaten.

As tepid as a fridge,
Storing food for the kids.

As chilly as a tap,
Carrying water right out.

Michael Chapman (9)
Settle Primary School, Settle

Temperature Poem

As cold as a snowflake, melting slowly in my warm hand,
As hot as a fire flame, burning paper which turns into ash,
As chilly as a penguin, shivering in the snow,
As boiling as soup with steam, slowly rising up.

Alice Jane Syms (7)
Settle Primary School, Settle

I'm Useless!

When I'm not concentrating,
I'm like glue without a stick,
A candle without a wick,
A president that's thick
And a budgie that got sick.

When I'm not concentrating,
I'm like an orange that is green,
A cake without cream,
A goblet with no gleam,
A football match with no teams.

When I'm not concentrating,
I'm like a garden without a flower,
A clock without an hour,
A house without a shower
And a castle without a tower.

When I'm not concentrating,
I'm like a table with no top,
A road without a stop,
Goodies without a shop,
A police force without a cop.

When I'm not concentrating . . .

Nathan Moore (10)
South Milford CP School, Leeds

The Magic Box

(Based on 'Magic Box' by Kit Wright)

I will put in my magic box . . .

A dragon flying over the moon,
Leaving a magical rainbow in the sky,
The sound of the wind like a harp in motion,
The golden sand glistening in the bright sun.

I will put in my magic box . . .

A brown tree covered in chocolate,
Which will never be finished,
The waves like white horses galloping onto the sand.

I will put in my magic box . . .

The biggest ship in the world,
A poisonous ladybird in a box,
A blind pigeon which can't fly
And the sky with no clouds.

That is what I will put in my magic box!

Nick Jones (11)
South Milford CP School, Leeds

Frog's Creation

(Based on 'Cat Began' by Andrew Matthews)

Frog
Took the colour from the grass
Pinched the croak of a chesty cough
Borrowed the tongue of an anteater
Grabbed the leap of a kangaroo
Stole the eyes from an owl . . .
The frog was created.

Jack Baddon (10)
South Milford CP School, Leeds

Tiger Of The Sea

The sea is a tiger scratching its
Prey like the sea hitting the cliff.

The sea is a tiger roaring like the
Sea making its wave.

The sea is a tiger smashing through
The caves leaving an arch.

The sea is a tiger during the day when the
Tiger is calm and the waves are soft,
But at night the tiger starts to crash
And the waves appear.

The sea is a tiger scratching the shore,
But when the tiger jumps the shore gets big and
Powerful, but now the tiger is calm -
Like the waves of the sea.

Billy Cheng (10)
South Milford CP School, Leeds

The Magic Box

(Based on 'Magic Box' by Kit Wright)

I will put in my box . . .
A leprechaun climbing a rainbow
A giant yellow sun turning black
A flow of rain making a tornado.

I will put in my box . . .
A jet picking up people in a net
An escaping fish from a shark
A flying catfish falling from the sky.

I will put in my box . . .
Gold turning into ice cream
A jaguar jumping on one leg
A dog skating on ice.

Harrie Mosey (11)
South Milford CP School, Leeds

Dinner Disaster

Lesley Light,
Had frand-o-bite,
Made from custard and beans,
Luther Brickle,
Ate rhubarb and pickle,
Bursting at the seams.

Diana Seat,
Had frosted meat,
Topped with strawberry glue,
Anthony Labbage,
Ate jam-covered cabbage,
Which sunk in a sauce of
Green goo.

After dinner was served,
They got what they deserved,
They were sick on their empty plate,
But everyone said,
Don't send them to bed,
Because death will come to them as fate.

Emilia Fuisdale (11)
South Milford CP School, Leeds

When I Am Not Concentrating

When I am not concentrating I am as useless as . . .

A bird with no wings,
A dog with no bark,
A spider with no web,
A horse with no gallop,
A fish with no fins,
A tiger with no stripes
And a solar system with no planets -
So I will start concentrating!

Luke Rowling (11)
South Milford CP School, Leeds

The Sea Dragon

I am the hungry sea dragon
I open my dark eye
And a storm starts
I lash my tail along the cliffs
And dig my teeth into the sand
When I'm angry I'll stamp about
And rough pounding waves will come
When I'm calm I'll swish my tail
And soft ripples will start
When I'm hungry
I'll lap up ships
Swallow the sand
And gobble pebbles.

I am the hungry sea dragon
I open my mouth
And my spit drowns the houses
I stand up and cause a tsunami
And strike my spikes into caves
When I'm sad I'll stomp
And raging waves begin
When I'm happy I'll breathe fire
And the sea will be warm
When I'm sleepy
I'll lay down, turn on my side
And bring in the tide.

Beatrice Mills (11)
South Milford CP School, Leeds

Giraffe Created

(Based on 'Cat Began' by Andrew Matthews)

It stole the colour
Of the sun,

And the shape
Of a rock,
For its coat.

The giraffe also copied,
The gracefulness,
Of a tree wobbling,
Proudly,
For its movement.

It snatched,
The ears of an ogre,
The sun made them yellow.

The giraffe borrowed,
The height of a cliff,
For its neck.

The giraffe took,
The swoopingness from an
Elephant's trunk,
For its tail.

And that is how the giraffe was created.

Beth Marchant (10)
South Milford CP School, Leeds

The Sea Dragon

I am the sea dragon,
My tail causes devastation to the
People at the beach
My fiery breath clashes against
The sea wall.

My anger is so powerful it can
Cause a tsunami
Under the sea everyone hates me
In summer I sunbathe
In winter I am provoked
Which causes my fury.

I am the sea dragon,
My beaming eyes lock onto the sea
I gobble up the sand wherever I can
I watch surfers in anger and
Swallow them in one go
I blow strong and the kites go high
I see people running away
I am the sea dragon!

Samuel Bryan (10)
South Milford CP School, Leeds

The Sea Horse

I am a sea horse galloping on the sand
With graceful energy when I am calm.

But when I am angry my mane swishes
And sways with furious movement.

The waves are strong, devouring anything in my way,
My whinny crashes against the sea wall.

I rear as I approach the shore
But now I am calm and tired . . .
I fetch the tide in.

Siân Harrison (10)
South Milford CP School, Leeds

The Raging Dog

The sea is a dog of raging madness,
It smashes along the beach all day,
Tearing up the seaweed from the seabed.

The sea is a dog of raging madness,
The white teeth of the waves sharply run along the rocks.

The sea is a dog of raging madness,
It guards the beach and swallows the leftover sand.

The sea is a dog of raging madness,
It feasts on the leftover cliffs.

The sea is a dog of dreaming wonders,
It rolls on the shore, leaving a trail of prints behind.

Hayley Lewis (11)
South Milford CP School, Leeds

The Birth Of A Cheetah

(Based on 'Cat Began' by Andrew Matthews)

He stole the speed of a Ferrari
And grabbed the swiftness of the wind
So his claws were made

He borrowed the blade of a knife
And took the glimpse of the moon
And his teeth were made

He gathered dabs of ink
And snatched the colour of the sun
And his coat was made

He swiped the colour of the ocean
And he pinched the sharpness of broken glass
And the cheetah was made.

Sean Arron Stubbs (10)
South Milford CP School, Leeds

The Hungry Sea Bear

I am the hungry sea
On a stormy day,
Swallowing the fish,
Breaking up the sand,
As I'm rolling to the shore,
The wind makes it sound like I'm roaring,
I am starving, eating everything,
I am calm when my tummy is full,
I am calm now!

I was the hungry sea bear,
I am the calm sea bear, rolling back into the sea,
Playing with the fish that I have missed,
I am sorted now
I am the calm sea bear.

Siobhan Wragg (10)
South Milford CP School, Leeds

My Magic Box
(Based on 'Magic Box' by Kit Wright)

In my magic box I will put . . .
A fierce killer whale doing heart surgery on a fish,
The bright sun and the magical marvellous moon,
Having a chat, eating ice cream,
The reflection of the beautiful stars in the shiny sparkling sea,
The shadows of the fluffy clouds floating in the silhouette
                                    of the fire-lit sky,
A frozen snowman drinking a Slush Puppy
                        on a delightful summer's day,
A teacher running a shop and a shopkeeper looking after a class of 27,
The greatest ray of sunlight and the brightest light of a northern star,
The biggest football that was blown up by the largest tornado,
I will put on my box . . .
A lock to keep my secrets safe.

Matt Wilkinson (10)
South Milford CP School, Leeds

The Giraffe Found

(Based on 'Cat Began' by Andrew Matthews)

She borrowed the carefulness of a spy to make her movement,
She pinched the length of a tightrope to make her long neck,
She took the bright yellow colour from the hot desert sun
                              to make the base of her coat,
She took brown splodges of an artist's paintbrush
                              to complete her coat,
She stole the curviness of a kitchen spoon to create her tongue,
She picked a twig off the ground to form her tail,
She drank the waves from the sea to make her tail sway,
She broke the height of trees to get the length of her legs,
She stole black marbles to create her beady eyes,
She nicked the fur off a horse's mane to make her own,
She nicked the muzzle from the lion to create her own,
She swiped two triangles from a homework sheet,
                              to form her own ears,
She gathered the weight of a bird's feather to make her steady pace.

The giraffe has found her body, she is now complete.

Katie Buckthorpe (11)
South Milford CP School, Leeds

The Blonde d'Aquitaine

The Blonde as it's usually referred to,
Is a cow, a big one at that.
Standing in a show ring,
Looking so proud,
Or in the shed with a newborn calf.
The tension of the sale ring,
When the prices are high,
Or the happiness of an owner,
When his bull wins a prize.
That's the Blonde d'Aquitaine.

Patrick Armitage (11)
Sutton-Upon-Derwent CE Primary School, York

The Hackney And The Dales

Look at that hackney,
How proud it looks,
Its soft hair smells as nice as roses
And its mane and tail are really thick,
But the dales pony is my favourite,
Its lovely thick hair has a sweet fragrance,
With its lovely temper,
It's the best in the world!

Elizabeth Gray (10)
Sutton-Upon-Derwent CE Primary School, York

These I Have Loved

The high-pitch mewl of an electric guitar,
The thundering of tornadoes,
The booming of a Ducati,
The crunching of leaves,
As they fall off the trees.
The swishing of waves,
The crashing of rocks,
The roughness of the sea,
The leaping of fish
And the squawking of seagulls,
As they fly over the sea.

Sam Holme (11)
Sutton-Upon-Derwent CE Primary School, York

These I Have Loved

I like the sound of the tractor drilling
And the smell the engine gives when the New Holland boils up,
The smell of the red diesel as I fill up the tractor,
But especially the dust that gets chucked up when I start drilling.

Ryan Bailey (11)
Sutton-Upon-Derwent CE Primary School, York

These I Have Loved

The people in the crowd talking and birds singing overhead
And the wind whistles through the crowd
And at the seaside the birds squawking
And people talking, eating, shopping,
It is the best place to be
And something else I have forgotten,
The waves lapping each other like they were having a fight
And farmers were coming up and down with their tractors,
I like the sound of my family being happy.

Megan Burrow (7)
Sutton-Upon-Derwent CE Primary School, York

These I Have Loved

Diggers are chugging
Tractors ploughing up the rutty field
Trucks tip in the tipping yard
Shotguns bang in the field
Motorbikes roar down the road
Machinery clanking in the factory
Cows mooing in the field
Chickens in the hut
A dog in the house, barking.

Jon-Ross Richardson (7)
Sutton-Upon-Derwent CE Primary School, York

The Dalmatian

The spotty Dalmatian lies in a field,
The spotty Dalmatian walks slowly,
The spotty Dalmatian yelps so loud,
The spotty Dalmatian goes mad,
The spotty Dalmatian goes home to bed.

Jake Dunn (9)
Sutton-Upon-Derwent CE Primary School, York

What I Like To Hear

Dogs barking,
Cats purring like an engine chugging,
Tractors rowing over the bumps in the field,
Piglets squeaking like little mice,
Cows mooing like something bellowing,
Ponies' hooves clip-clopping,
It sounds funny, hens clucking and ducks quacking,
Birds singing like a piano playing.

Lauren Gill (8)
Sutton-Upon-Derwent CE Primary School, York

The Haunted Ship

The ship is big and very stiff,
The ship creaks when it moves,
The ship is haunted by a ghost,
The ship is lonely on the bay,
The ship has no crew, nobody knows why,
The ship is covered in fog,
The ship has a curse that kills everyone who goes near it,
The ship is owned by the spirits of the town.

Alex Draycott (8)
Sutton-Upon-Derwent CE Primary School, York

These Things I Like To Hear

I like the sound of birds twittering in my ear,
The whistling of the wind rushing through the branches,
The seagulls squawking at the seaside, fighting over food,
The waves roaring and lapping onto the shore,
The rustle of the leaves when children jump into them.

Gemma Burrow (10)
Sutton-Upon-Derwent CE Primary School, York

My Dreams

Loving a horse, riding round and round,
Hating my time in a crocodile's mouth,
Packing my bags as I run through the door,
Taking over my mum and dad.

Juggling on a clown's head,
Really scared in my bed,
Catch my breath,
Go to sleep.

The doctor walks through the door,
Needles poke me through the knee,
Love is all while I sleep,
Shivering I'm so scared.

Bethany Warren (8)
Sutton-Upon-Derwent CE Primary School, York

The Mysterious Creature!

He swoops over the treetops,
His shadow lies behind him,
His great feathery wings flapping,
His long legs kicking the air,
Getting higher and higher,
His silver outline stands out,
In the night sky,
His horn, lined with glitter, pointing in front of him,
His white slender body shining in the moonlight,
Flying past houses and fields, roads and woods
And that was the last I saw of him,
The mighty unicorn.

Megan Letts (9)
Sutton-Upon-Derwent CE Primary School, York

When I Grow Up

When I grow up
I want a Lamborghini
It goes at 500 miles per hour
It has got a lot of power
It has a roof that opens up wide
You press a button from inside
It'll be white with black leather seats
No one will be allowed sticky sweets
When I grow up
I want a Lamborghini.

Ross Houlihan (8)
Valewood Primary School, Crosby

Stay In Touch

A lazy teenager called Joan
Never bothered to pick up the phone
So she missed out on dates
Lost touch with her mates
And spent every evening alone.

Sally Hayes-May (9)
Valewood Primary School, Crosby

What Is Black?

What is black?
The night is black,
With Father Christmas and his sack!

What is gold?
Money is gold,
So big and bright and bold!

What is white?
Seagulls are white,
Flying in broad daylight!

Olivia Yoxall (9)
Valewood Primary School, Crosby

Cat In The Hat

There was an old lady
Who had a fat cat
Who loved to sleep in her best hat.
One day there was a knock on the door
The wind blew in and the hat fell on the floor.
The cat fell out but not on its own,
A family of kittens had made it their home.

Nicola Smeaton (9)
Valewood Primary School, Crosby

Frog Hops

One hop, two hops,
I'm a little frog

Three hop, four hops,
Flopping on a log

Five hop, six hops,
That's the way to bop

Seven hop, eight hops,
Wheeeee! Plop.

Felipe Davis-Guzman (8)
Valewood Primary School, Crosby

There Was A Young Croc Named Snap

There was a young croc named Snap,
Who had an ancient map,
His mum ripped it up,
He cried like a pup
And hurt his mum with his cap.

Stephanie Taylor (9)
Valewood Primary School, Crosby

What Is?

What is blue?
The sky is blue,
With birds flying through.

What is red?
Blood is red,
Flowing through your body
To your head.

Max Forden (8)
Valewood Primary School, Crosby

The House

The radiator gurgled
As it was turned on full heat,
The clock hesitated
Before ticking on.
The rocking chair groaned
As the fat old woman slumped down on it,
The bed snarled as the child
Jumped on it.
The coffee table screamed
As the woman spilt coffee on it,
The bin laughed as the man
Fed it with rotten rubbish.

Charly Redmond (11)
Westholme Middle School, Blackburn

The Park

The leaves pranced around the air,
While roundabouts danced with laughing children.
Swings creaked in the wind,
Benches groaned while children jumped on them.
The slide spat the fat child out and made him cry,
Sandpits cried when children dug out their contents.

Alice Holland (10)
Westholme Middle School, Blackburn

The Seaside

The waves danced on the seashore,
The wind whistled through the palm trees,
Panic pinched her
As the shark came up behind her.

Sand ran around the shore,
As the stones sat silently in the water,
The umbrellas waved in the breeze,
The sandcastles breathed through their little holes.

The shells chattered in the cold, cold sea,
The dustbins gobbled up scraps,
Sand sneaked into the children's sandwiches,
The pebbles drank the sea water.

Holly Adamson (11)
Westholme Middle School, Blackburn

The Football Match

The tunnel spits out
The players, one by one.

The whistle screams
As the ball is kicked.

The pitch starts to groan
As the players run about.

The ball bounces
Up and down.

Hot dog buns smile
As the hot dog wiggles inside them.

Bins catch the rubbish
Thrown at them.

The football stand
Is now asleep.

Charlotte Stockwell (11)
Westholme Middle School, Blackburn

If My Thoughts Took Shape

If my brave thoughts took shape
They would be like me fighting
In the world war.

If my proud thoughts took shape
I would be getting a medal
From the Queen.

If my bossy thoughts took shape
I would be shouting
At my sisters.

If my imaginative thoughts took shape
I would be in chocolate heaven
Floating on a chocolate river.

If my silly thoughts took shape
I would be a clown
On a tightrope.

If my peaceful thoughts took shape
I would be a dove as white as snow
Gliding in the air.

Heather Duckworth (10)
Westholme Middle School, Blackburn

On The Beach

Palm trees dance in the sunlight,
The sand whispers across the beach,
The sea tosses onto the shore,
The seashells roll on the golden sand.

Seaweed slithers on the coast,
Rocks jump into the sea,
The sun yawns as it sets in the sky,
Now the beach will sleep till the new day comes.

Malini Dey (10)
Westholme Middle School, Blackburn

Mysterious Sounds

I listened to an empty bottle
And thought I could hear,
The sound of the sea groaning
And running through my ear.

I held a hollow shell,
Close against my head,
At night thunder,
Booming round my bed.

I found a dried-up leaf
And listened for a sound,
I thought I heard the rustling,
Of small animals on the ground.

I found an empty bird cage
And walked up to it with no fear,
I thought I heard a parrot,
Screeching in my ear.

Lucy Janus (10)
Westholme Middle School, Blackburn

Sounds Like . . .

I took an empty kettle
To see what I might hear
And thought I heard a pixie's voice
Whispering in my ear.

I found an empty sweet box
And listened for a sound
I thought I heard a giant
Stamping on the ground.

I heard a clip file close
It sounded very clear
Almost like a chicken cluck
Right against my ear.

Martha Hindle (10)
Westholme Middle School, Blackburn

If My Thoughts Took Shape

If my daring thoughts took shape
They would be like someone
Jumping into the North Sea!

If my peaceful thoughts took shape
They would be like someone
Sitting quietly, reading a book!

If my proud thoughts took shape
I would have just got a gold
In the Olympics for gymnastics!

If my lazy thoughts took shape
They would be like someone
Asleep in bed!

If my funny thoughts took shape
They would be like someone dancing
The cancan while dressed as a clown!

If my selfish thoughts took shape
I wouldn't tell you
Even if you begged me!

Last of all . . .

If my favourite thoughts took shape
I would be sitting on a stool
With the sorting hat low over my head!

Klara Holmes (10)
Westholme Middle School, Blackburn

If My Thoughts Took Shape

If my sad thoughts took shape
I would cry
A river of tears.

If my imaginative thoughts took shape
I would be a book character
Trapped between the pages.

If my calm thoughts took shape
I would be in a spa
Having a pedicure.

If my proud thoughts took shape
I would have created
World peace.

If my scary thoughts took shape
I would sleep with the light on
So the ghosts couldn't get me.

If my lazy thoughts took shape
I would be a man sitting on the settee
Watching the TV and eating chocolate.

If my romantic thoughts took shape
I would be on my honeymoon
Watching the sunset on the sea
And I would never want to leave.

Abigail Hindley (10)
Westholme Middle School, Blackburn

Spring

When spring wakes up,
Her fingertips push through the soil,
She dances and beckons,
Some flowers up to the surface,
Wherever her feet touch the ground,
Little flowers burst up around her,
She gestures her hand to a tree,
The tree flourishes,
She starts to sing her sweet serenade,
The birds have an urge to join in,
She kisses the buds,
Then licks them to make them sticky,
She wanders over to where the animals are,
She tickles the roe deer to awake him,
She whispers in the ear of the rabbit
And she taps a boar,
All is well and all is happy.

Lauren Waterhouse (10)
Westholme Middle School, Blackburn

Glad Is Spring

She rises upon the ground
And every step she takes
A blossoming bluebell
Rises upon the ground
And all the gardens are green
With snowbells
All the reindeer prancing
In the beautiful garden
Glad is spring
She gently falls back to sleep
For the spring to end
And the summer to come once again.

Lydia Sage (10)
Westholme Middle School, Blackburn

If My Thoughts Took Shape

If my imaginative thoughts took shape
There would be
A pig flying by.

If my daring thoughts took shape
I would be
Jumping off a cloud.

If my lazy thoughts took shape
I would be
Asleep all through the day.

If my graceful thoughts took shape
I would be
Skating on a shiny lake.

If my peaceful thoughts took shape
I would be
Sailing a river in an elegant white gown.

If my loving thoughts took shape
I would be
Giving presents to the world.

Melissa Duffy (10)
Westholme Middle School, Blackburn

Spring

Spring slowly opens her dainty eyes,
Out of her cave, she swiftly flies,
She tickles the squirrels and the deer,
She whispers into the bear's soft ears,
But she never has any fear,
Now the birds all start to hear
And sing to rejoice that spring is here!

Laura Meredith Hallam (10)
Westholme Middle School, Blackburn

If My Thoughts Took Shape

If my peaceful thoughts took shape
I would be paragliding over the Mediterranean Sea
Looking over all of Cyprus.

If my daring thoughts took shape
I would be going on The Big One
Ten times, non-stop.

If my brave thoughts took shape
I would be fighting a lion in the jungle
With snakes all around me.

If my romantic thoughts took shape
I would be riding a swan, humming songs of all kinds
Then slowly drifting off to sleep.

If my lazy thoughts took shape
I would be lying on the sofa watching television
And eating as much chocolate as I could.

If my proud thoughts took shape
I would be winning the hurdles gold medal
At the Olympics.

Gabrielle Lamoury (10)
Westholme Middle School, Blackburn

Spring

Spring awakes eventually
The flowers pop open as she walks by
The buds awake when she touches them
The ice disappears as she smiles
The grass reappears when she walks on it
She walks as gently as a fairy.

Rosie Hewson-Jones (9)
Westholme Middle School, Blackburn

If My Thoughts Took Shape

If my tranquil thoughts took shape
I would be asleep in a tree
Dreaming happy thoughts.

If my melancholic thoughts took shape
I would be sitting in the corner
Of an orphanage.

If my silly thoughts took shape
I would be a clown
Getting a pie in the face.

If my unusual thoughts took shape
I would be walking
In a never-ending estate.

If my imaginative thoughts took shape
I would be a fairy riding a unicorn
Through a mystical wood.

If my mischievous thoughts took shape
I would be a spy
For the government.

Amy Panchoo (11)
Westholme Middle School, Blackburn

Flaming Fireworks

As I peep from my bedroom window into the dark night sky,
I see a flaming firework drifting down to die.
It's the 5th of November, it's Bonfire Night
And as I watch the flaming bonfire, it lights up the pitch-black sky
And . . . then . . . I hear a squeaking sound and after that . . .
There's a cry, *'A banger!'*
And then I jumped back into bed, sleepy but excited!
I'd actually watched a bonfire display without even going to one!

Emily Wright (7)
Westholme Middle School, Blackburn

If My Thoughts Took Shape

If my peaceful thoughts took shape
I would be meditating in mountain air
Everyone will help each other
Everyone will share.

If my fearful thoughts took shape
I would be in a darkened room
Surrounded by evil monsters
Awaiting my doom.

If my sulky thoughts took shape
I would always be in a mood
I would always shout and be unkind
Just like Mr Scrooge.

If my imaginative thoughts took shape
I would be able to fly
I would see the birds and butterflies
While soaring through the sunny sky.

If my lazy thoughts took shape
I wouldn't do my homework, I'd just have fun.
If my lazy thoughts took shape
This poem would not be written and done!

Zyra Shah (11)
Westholme Middle School, Blackburn

If My Thoughts Took Shape

If my difficult thoughts took shape
They would be like a person
Struggling to reach the top of Mount Everest.

If my frightening thoughts took shape
They would be me crossing a rocky, wooden bridge
Above a pool of sharks.

If my romantic thoughts took shape
They would be sitting by a moonlit lake
Watching the stars go by.

If my fantasy thoughts took shape
They would be like living in a world
Full of elves, dwarves and fairies.

If my adventurous thoughts took shape
They would be like swinging
Through the trees of the rainforest.

If my melancholic thoughts took shape
They would be like my parents
Sending me to an orphanage.

If my favourite thoughts took shape
They would be like winning the 800m
At the Olympic Games.

Georgina Butler (10)
Westholme Middle School, Blackburn

If My Thoughts Took Shape

If my peaceful thoughts took shape
They would be like rowing down a rippling river
Surrounded by the countryside.

If my adventurous thoughts took shape
They would be like crossing a rickety bridge
In the middle of a safari.

If my furious thoughts took shape
They would be like the whole world
Being set on fire.

If my proud thoughts took shape
They would be like
Lying on a bed of trophies.

If my noisy thoughts took shape
They would be like a stampede of elephants
Running through a china shop.

If my imaginative thoughts took shape
They would be like
Raining cats and dogs.

Eleanor Lynch (11)
Westholme Middle School, Blackburn

The Writer Of This Poem

(Based on 'The Writer of this Poem' by Roger McGough)

The writer of this poem
Is as tall as can be
As strong as a giant
Squeezy as can be

Loves the taste of chocolate
Likes to watch TV
But hates to have her tea

As straight as a gate
As cute as a mouse
Cool as ice
As clean as a cleaner
Sharp as a nail

Flexible as a gymnast
Stubby as a cabbage
Kind as a teacher
And hates the taste of grapefruit

She's one in a million billion
(Or so the poem says).

Bronwyn Richards (8)
Westholme Middle School, Blackburn

The Writer Of This Poem

(Based on 'The Writer of this Poem' by Roger McGough)

The writer of this poem
Can be as small as a mouse
Maybe as big as a crowd
Or as tall as a house

The writer of this poem
Is as kind as the elderly
Sometimes as calm as the sea
Or as busy as a bee

The writer of this poem
Is as cheeky as a monkey
As chatty as a parrot
And as hard-working as a donkey

The writer of this poem
Is as suspicious as can be
The writer of this poem
Is a mystery to you and me.

Salonee Shah (7)
Westholme Middle School, Blackburn

Bonfire Night

Fireworks burst into the night sky
And fall down to Earth in golden showers.

Catherine wheel, how I adore your spin,
As you spit out orange and red fire.

Roman candle, everyone laughs and cheers,
To see you squirt out spectacular tears.

Oh rocket, as you make your drilling sound
And burst into the cold air of the night sky.

Oh sparkler, how tempting it is to see you glow,
Your fantastic, wonderful, golden glow,
How I wish you would go on forever!

Lucia Lamoury (7)
Westholme Middle School, Blackburn

Summer Sounds

Willows weeping
But never know to cry
I put my head in the hollow
And hear a continuing sigh.

Golden meadows swaying in the breeze
My ear to a burrow in the ground
I hear rabbits' paws
Scampering round and round.

Owls hooting
An eggshell in a nest
I climb up to see
A chick hatching from its rest.

I walk into more woodland
And look up into the sky
I close my eyes and listen
To the wind's sweet song way up high.

Harriet Allardyce (10)
Westholme Middle School, Blackburn

Firework Demonstration

Catherine wheels are whizzing
And rockets go *bang!* way up high!
Everyone cheering and laughing,
Holding sparklers, writing their name in the sky.

My eardrums are popping with laughter,
Glowing embers lie by the fire.
Fireworks go *whiz, pop, bang, crackle!*
Rockets fly higher and higher.

Now the bonfire is just ashes,
We say goodbye to our friends.
I really enjoyed all the fireworks,
But now it's all come to an end.

Annabel Steele (7)
Westholme Middle School, Blackburn

Magic Things

I found a little poppy
And all I could hear
Was the sound of big bombs
Blasting right through my ear.

I found a little toy bird
And all that I could see
Was a little bird singing so sweetly
Just sitting right beside me.

I found a little flower
And all I could smell
Was the flower I loved
Which was called bluebell.

I found a little kitten
And all I could feel
Was the soft and fluffy fur
And she was eating her meal.

Heera Hussain (10)
Westholme Middle School, Blackburn

Spring Queen

She awakes gracefully
Upon a comfy cloud
She gets in her golden chariot
And rides to Earth
She points at a dark cloud
And it turns into the sun
Wherever her pale white feet go
Flowers start to grow
She touches some eggs
They hatch, amazingly
Wherever she walks
Things hatch, sprout and grow
Then she goes to sleep again
Until Earth needs her again.

Hattie Campbell (10)
Westholme Middle School, Blackburn

The Writer Of This Poem

(Based on 'The Writer of this Poem' by Roger McGough)

The writer of this poem
Is small but yet affective
And she can be connected

She can bite
She can write
And is a beautiful sight
She is as slow
As a snail
(Her writing I mean)

She is an animal lover
For all different species
Her hair is long and fair

She doesn't care what it looks like
She loves getting muddy
Dirty and wet
She loves her life so far
She's one in a million.

Maddison Ainsworth (8)
Westholme Middle School, Blackburn

Spring

Spring suddenly opens her sky-blue eyes
Out of Fairy Land she flies
With a catkin she combs her hair
And out of the dew pops a pear
From the bare, thin trees
Emerges fresh green leaves
With all her fairy power
She changes an old leaf into a flower
Gives a deer a tap on his nose
And on she goes.

Sophie Louise Greenall (10)
Westholme Middle School, Blackburn

My Imagination

I walked up to a little door
And looked straight through the keyhole.
I thought I saw a growling monster,
In a cave as black as coal.

I put my ear to a radiator,
To listen to the sound.
It came out as a crackling noise,
That dug into the ground.

I listened to a ticking clock,
Which sounded very queer.
It sounded like a newborn chick
Pecking at my ear.

I picked up a water bottle
And put it by my ear.
It sounded like the whooshing sea,
That is what I hear.

Charlotte Anne Flood (10)
Westholme Middle School, Blackburn

My Poem

I found an empty bottle
Lying by the garden rake
I picked it up and listened
And heard water gushing in a lake.

I was looking for a knife and fork
In the kitchen drawer
And when I opened it so wide
I heard a sudden roar.

I found a little pebble
Just there upon the ground
I put it to my ear
And heard a pretty chirping sound.

Stephanie Jane Leaver (10)
Westholme Middle School, Blackburn

Spring

Spring arises from her sleep,
Making all the birdies cheep,
With her lovely song so sweet,
Gets animals up on their feet.

Daffodils and tulips gracefully grow,
With all the other plants that spring will sow,
Overgrown grass the girl will mow,
Spring is a lovely person, you know.

Did I tell about the dewdrops?
Your garden gets as wet as mops,
I think an elf inside a plane drops,
Buckets of water, but makes no plops.

But now spring is over and summer arrives,
Which drives the young lady back to sleep-life,
At lease she still says all her goodbyes,
Then she'll lie down and gently close her eyes.

Amelia Deakin (10)
Westholme Middle School, Blackburn

Listening

I found an empty cage
And I approached with no fear
I thought I heard a cat
Scratching at its ear.

I listened to a seashell
And I thought I heard the waves
Splashing high on the beach
And echoing in a cave.

I held an empty cup
To see what I could hear
I thought I heard a person
Whispering in my ear.

Charlotte Amber Pattison (10)
Westholme Middle School, Blackburn

Spring

Spring has popped her head out of her cave,
She gives her delicate wand a wave.
To make the snowy blanket disappear,
So crows and blackbirds she can hear.
She swiftly tiptoes to the pond
And frogspawn appears with a flick of her wand.
Now off she skips to the fields,
So she can wake the animals.
Over to the squirrels she goes
And gives them all a tickle on their nose.
Now they awake and follow Spring,
They help her kiss the buds to make flowers
And discover all Spring's powers.
Now Spring invites them all to tea,
They watch the butterflies and the bees.

Sophie Ahmed (9)
Westholme Middle School, Blackburn

Hearing Sounds Of Magic

I found an empty snail shell
Then put it to my ear
I heard the sound of music
So very loud and clear.

I took a shiny pebble
And listened for a sound
I'm sure I heard the noise of mice
Running on the ground.

I put my ear to a leaf
And what I heard was this:
The sound of tweeting birds
Blowing me a kiss!

Sophie Ludlam (10)
Westholme Middle School, Blackburn

The Spring Fairy

Under a bud
Beneath the ground
Lies a spring fairy
Waiting to flutter around
She stretches out her arms
To the tips of her fingers
Then spreads out her wings
And flutters up to see us
She looks around
And sees nothing
But some dry old leaves
And a farmer's hut
She searches the meadows
High and low
Then thinks to herself
Where do the animals go?
She runs to the forest
They're sure to be there
And there she finds
A badger and bear.

Rachel Martin (9)
Westholme Middle School, Blackburn

Sports Poem

Basketball, basketball, bounce, bounce, bounce
Basketball, basketball, bounce on the ground.

Skipping, skipping, tap, tap, tap
Skipping, skipping, tap it on the ground.

Running, running, running in the yard
Running, running, run and have fun.

Football, football, yeah! I scored a goal
Football, football, kick it, off you go.

Playtime's over, go and line up
Playtime's over, got to wait till lunch.

Then we will come out and do it all again
Yippee! Yippee! Can't wait till then!

Alexandra Kerry Edge (10)
Westways Primary School, Sheffield

Contrasts Of War

Danger is full of dirt and mud,
It's full of dying bodies and blood,
Safe is where you're in a happy place,
Seeing a smile on everybody's face.

Danger is war far away,
Nobody wants to go, nobody wants to stay,
But safe is what makes the world go round,
No war or crashing, just a peaceful sound.

Danger makes children cry,
No happiness, just people made to die,
Safe is the road to joy,
Brings a smile to every girl and boy.

Maddie Hartley (10)
Woodlands Junior School, Harrogate

A Graveyard

Graveyards are lonely,
Always speaking to themselves,
Trying not to cry,
Always bringing arrivals,
People leaving families.

Joshua Kirk (10)
Woodlands Junior School, Harrogate

Fire Flames

Its flames burning the room
Bright, warm, roaring
As bright as the sun
Like a big spark blowing in my face
Makes me feel evil and bad
Feels like I'm in Hell
Reminds me of the danger there will be!

Jessica Murray (11)
Woodlands Junior School, Harrogate

The Eagle's Hunt

The great eagle strikes
Diving, gliding at the lamb
The hunt of the lamb
Outstretched talons wait to kill
Ready to feast on its flesh.

Christopher Sheldon (10)
Woodlands Junior School, Harrogate

A Soldier's Son, A Message From His Heart

I wish my dad didn't meet death,
I wish my father never left,
I wish he didn't rise above,
I want to give him all my love.

I wish people didn't cry,
I wish people didn't die,
I wish everyone healthy and fit,
I wish war would just quit.

I wish war would never come,
I would we could play and have fun,
I wish death couldn't be,
I wish we were free for eternity.

I wish we didn't go away,
I wish we could just play,
I wish we could just go home,
I wish I didn't have to groan.

I wish this was a dream,
I wish war wasn't mean,
I wish it was calm and quiet,
I wish there wasn't a big riot.

I wish my mum and dad were here,
I just have to shed a tear,
It is tearing a hole inside my brain,
That I can't see them again.

James Devall (11)
Woodlands Junior School, Harrogate

Blitz

Sirens beginning to wail and roar,
I've never seen a war like this before.
Smoke is everywhere and I'm sad,
I've lost my family and now I'm mad.

Fatlum Ibrahimi (11)
Woodlands Junior School, Harrogate

Evacuee

Home is cold and frightening
Home is uninviting
Away there are cows and sheep
Away is where I can sleep.

Home is full of people dying
Home is full of families crying
Away is happy, not sad
Away is good, not bad.

Home is full of trenches muddy
Home is dark, gloomy and muddy
Away is dreamy and funny
Away is peaceful and sunny.

Home is where everyone fights
Home is where you can't sleep at night
Away is safe for me to play
Away is where I have fun day after day.

Freya Johnson (11)
Woodlands Junior School, Harrogate

The Mighty Dragon - Tankas

The mighty dragon
A huge and scaly reptile
With razor-sharp claws
Its huge wings wave rapidly
Sharp spikes run down its huge back.

His amazing strength
His flame destroys anything
Its red flame destroys
Its luminous red eyes glow
In the cold, starry night sky.

James Turner (11)
Woodlands Junior School, Harrogate

The Elegant Phoenix

The elegant phoenix,
Very bright and special,
Big, strong, powerful,
Like a beautiful angel,
Like a giant silk-covered kite,
I feel jealous,
As if I am nothing compared to it,
The elegant phoenix,
The greatest thing in history.

James Dickinson (10)
Woodlands Junior School, Harrogate

Jet

Lost in the white sky
Blue sky in the horizon
Storm getting closer
Small jet getting blown away
Stormy sky is getting dark.

Harry Aitken (10)
Woodlands Junior School, Harrogate

Fierce Lion

Fierce lion
Ever so dangerous
Fierce, indestructible, wild
With eyes that look like roaring fire
Its mane like an electrified haystack
It makes me feel vulnerable
Like a fly caught in a spider's web
Fierce lion
Reminds us how life is short.

Faith Tagarira (10)
Woodlands Junior School, Harrogate

The Sudden Attack

It was a quiet night,
All the lights were off,
All you could see
Was black and white,
Like penguins standing in the open
Painted in stripes.

Suddenly, there was a bird-like shape,
Up in the sky,
Was it a bird?

Screaming! Shouting! Everywhere!
Bombers! Bombers dropping their deadly ware.

Sirens roaring like warning screams,
The bombers waiting for their victims
To return to their house of fears.

It's silent again
A small hand pokes
Out of the rubble
Reaching for hope.

It's all over
We have won . . . for now
But for how long?

Hannah Sumner (10)
Woodlands Junior School, Harrogate

The Great Tree

A beautiful tree
Swishing, swaying in the breeze
Like it's reaching out
Throughout the twists and turns
Of the vast sleepy forest.

Michael James Drake (11)
Woodlands Junior School, Harrogate

War Veterans

Men and women lost their lives,
So we could be here today,
We've listened to their stories,
Of their friends that passed away.

They slept in muddy ditches,
If they were lucky, a blanket to keep warm,
They took it in turns to sleep,
So no one would come to any harm.

My great-grandad was in the war
And had lots of stories to tell,
Some were very funny,
Some made him cry as well.

I always hold the door open,
For elderly men and women,
Because if it wasn't for them,
To school, I wouldn't be going.

Nicholas Scott Preston (11)
Woodlands Junior School, Harrogate

The Canon

The canon
Built long ago
Big, huge, scary
Like a plane roaring past
Like a fire crackling
It makes me feel small
Like a small beetle
The canon
You have not long to live.

Sam Colley (11)
Woodlands Junior School, Harrogate

No More War

I never wanted Earth to be at war,
Because it would just bring more and more,
Of loads of people dying and loads of people sighing,
That they never wanted Earth to be at war.

I never wanted Earth to be at war,
Because when I went outside, then I saw,
So many people dead and so many with no bed,
It is terrible, I tell you, with this war.

I never wanted Earth to be at war,
Because it really is far against the law,
It's really, really bad and I'm really, really sad,
With that annoying brain of Hitler's that's gone mad!

Fenella Walsh (10)
Woodlands Junior School, Harrogate

Blitz

Everywhere is black,
Hitler's ready for attack,
Sirens wailing with a roar,
Bombs smashing my front door.

All I can hear is people crying,
People dead and people dying,
The Germans attacking in the night,
We can't let Hitler win the fight.

Hitler's sending people to flight,
Over London so hang on tight,
Germany is here to make us die,
All their soldiers are in the sky.

Ryan Danby (10)
Woodlands Junior School, Harrogate

Blitz

The voice of terror in the sky
And hearing people cry, cry, cry,
When Hitler comes out of play,
He doesn't really know the way.

The sound of people in the night
And hearing people in a fright,
The sound of buildings falling down,
Chaos and destruction around the town.

Liam Caley (10)
Woodlands Junior School, Harrogate

Cath

There was a mechanic called Cath
Who tripped on the garden path
She ended up crying
Because she thought she was dying
Then she had a big laugh!

Thomas Lydon (10)
Woodlands Junior School, Harrogate

Blitz

I woke up to a deafening cry
When everyone's saying, 'Why, oh why?'
My mum and dad I truly love you
Please don't say I've lost you.

I go outside to a dreadful sight
Bombs dropped all through the night
Searching for my mum and dad
If they're dead I will be sad.

Sadie Gentle (10)
Woodlands Junior School, Harrogate

The Blackout

The blackout! The horrible blackout,
Especially when the guns start to shout!
I hope I make it through the night,
I don't want to go out in the dark and fight.

I hear a warden shout, 'Put out that light!'
Everybody's shaking with fright,
This is definitely Hell on Earth, all right,
As I hear the plane's predatory flight.

The bombs start to drop on us from high,
Boom! Bombs bang! We are all petrified,
It is over in a flash, the panthers are gone,
We have found a blown-up bomb.

The morning is here, no more bombs,
The war is won, we are victorious,
Victory! Victory! Victory! Is ours!
No more pain for us, or bombs.

Ryan Murphy (11)
Woodlands Junior School, Harrogate

Silver Dragon

A silver dragon,
Hundreds of years old.
Beautiful, sad, young,
Like the universe at night.
Like endless riches,
It makes me feel exhilarated.
Like a child at Christmas,
A silver dragon,
Reminds me that we will all get good luck.

Liam Shield (10)
Woodlands Junior School, Harrogate

The Blitz

When the blackout comes to town,
All our houses might crumble down,
Over comes the Devil's cloak
And now there is not much hope.

The bombs are raining to the ground
And all you can hear is a screaming sound,
Over comes the gigantic swarm,
This city will soon be torn.

Death is coming from the sky,
You'd better start running, you're going to die,
London is now a giant flame,
Don't go out, it isn't a game.

Adam Reel (10)
Woodlands Junior School, Harrogate

Nature

Animals leap high
Trees as big as giants
The sky is crystal clear

Jungle, a lively green
Parrots squawk awfully loud
Light green, dark green, brown

River flows gently
Fish jump high, touching the sky
Animals drink here

Jagged cliffs up high
Golden eagles watch their prey
Swoop down like lightning.

Chloe Wright (10)
Woodlands Junior School, Harrogate

Air Raid

War is coming
And the baby is crying,
All wives and girlfriends,
We're all sighing,
Men all marching through the town,
Left, right, up and down.

Air raids make a noisy yell,
Bombers send down a deadly shell,
ARP people shout,
'Put that flipping light out!'
Down in the shelter, in the garden,
People say that war needs a warden.

Peace has come, war has been,
Wives and girlfriends have seen,
Large letters in the news,
That their husbands and boyfriends have died,
See tears in their eyes,
For weeks and weeks you hear their cries.

Sarah McClean (11)
Woodlands Junior School, Harrogate

The Beautiful Cheetah

The cheetah
Sneaky, not noticed
Fast, vicious, wild
Like moving grass
Makes me feel sneaky
Like a cheetah not being seen
The beautiful cheetah
Makes me feel slow.

Alex Embleton (11)
Woodlands Junior School, Harrogate

We Want Peace

War is noisy, dark and frightening,
Soldiers fighting for their countries,
I want peace, not all this anger,
Peace is quiet, a safe place from danger.

War is trenches covered in mud,
Thousands of bodies covered in blood,
Peace is a place full of wonderful things,
A place I fly to on angel's wings.

War is dark, as black as night,
Even young men are expected to fight,
How many more lives will be lost?
At the end of the war we will count the cost.

Peace brings happiness all day long,
War is fatal and very, very wrong.

Tom Blackburn (10)
Woodlands Junior School, Harrogate

Peace

War is hated, people killing
War is unforgettable
Peace is lovely and peaceful
Peace is to be seen all around

War is bloody and terrible
War is horrible and scars its victims
Peace is a pool of togetherness
Peace should be all around

War is dismal, dark and muddy
War should no longer be around
Peace is beautiful, clean and quiet
Peace is a happy world.

Amy Wilson (11)
Woodlands Junior School, Harrogate

The Blackout

Blackout, blackout
As dark as you can think,
Put that light out,
The warden speaks.

Blackout, blackout,
As dark as death,
Scared of the night,
Hurry, hurry, out of breath.

Got to make it to the shelter,
Got to quickly find it,
Got to make it to the shelter,
Before the bombs begin to hit.

Why is there a blackout?
Is it because bombers are overhead,
From which we try to hide,
Before they drop and make us dead.

End of the blackout
Everyone is happy now,
We can put our lights on,
Until the night of tomorrow.

Chloe Jackson (11)
Woodlands Junior School, Harrogate

Cold Giver Wanted

We want someone to give us a cold
However, they cannot be bald
Maybe a cough or a sneeze
And possibly a freeze.

If you've got a disease
Give me it please
Just text 'sneeze' please to 34567.

Carl Linley (11)
Woodlands Junior School, Harrogate

A Sith Lord Required

A Sith Lord required,
With a long black cloak,
Are you ready to murder,
That dumb Jedi bloke?

Can you wield a sabre
Or throttle a clone?
Can you see the future,
Or whip up a cyclone?

Are you brave and strong?
With a heart of cold?
Are you clever and bold?
And are you not to be told?

Have you an electric eye?
And can you be independent?
Are you skilled in karate?
And are your forms relevant?

Then come to the forum,
At seven o'clock
And you may become feared,
As Lord Blanblock.

James Battle (11)
Woodlands Junior School, Harrogate

Trainee Wizard

Someone needed who is good at spells and potions
Not very old
With a pointy nose, pointy hat and a purple cape
If this is a job for you
Call me at 57890182 or text me at 88269
£15 per week.

Thomas Ferrol (11)
Woodlands Junior School, Harrogate

Peace To War

War is full of children's sad faces,
Children going to unknown places,
Peace is full of care and love,
Peace must come from up above.

War kills people,
Lots of people,
It's mean and hateful,
It is also extremely lethal.

Peace is fun,
There's no time to cry and run,
If peace was here, we would all sit
And talk under the sun.

Children return from the hills,
No more taking stress pills,
Peace will come back again,
Let's all play games and forget that threatening pain.

Samantha Laws (11)
Woodlands Junior School, Harrogate

Trees

Trees are very cool
They are all sorts of colours
And look very nice
When the wind blows
Leaves will fall
But then the leaves
Will grow back.

Duncan Stewart Halliday (10)
Woodlands Junior School, Harrogate

It's There!

Under my bed,
Under the stairs,
Everywhere I go,
Help! It's there!

It's big and hairy,
Yellow and green,
Leave me alone,
That's what I mean!

Then one day,
Behind me,
It was not there,
Or beside me,
Yes!

Georgina Normington (10)
Woodlands Junior School, Harrogate

Witchcraft

Nasty, evil witch
As old as the hills
Long, pointy nose
With warts on it
Wanted!

An expert at smelly spells
Must have an evil cackle
Owner of a splendid broomstick
And a bubbling cauldron
Wanted!

Greg Wallace (12)
Woodlands Junior School, Harrogate

Alice's Palace

There was a girl called Alice
She lived in a beautiful palace
She rode on a horse
And with great force
Fell heavily and broke her necklace.

Lilly Faye Coombes (11)
Woodlands Junior School, Harrogate

Ants - Haiku

Small, little creatures
Scurry along very fast
Back to their warm nest.

Jordan Faulkner (10)
Woodlands Junior School, Harrogate

Trainee Wizard

One trainee wizard
Pay will be great
We will not take people
Who are overweight
So please come down
To the wizard lab today
Interviews on Tuesday.

Paige Ellen Johnson (10)
Woodlands Junior School, Harrogate

Knight Wanted

Are you strong and fearless?
Like holding a sword?
Like wearing metal suits?
Knights always keep their word.

Not very old?
Not very young?
Around middle aged?
This could be for you!

If you're brave enough
Come to the interview!
You will need a war horse
This knight - it could be you!

If you could do all this
Open the doors
Come to see me
And it'll be yours!

Edward Darling (10)
Woodlands Junior School, Harrogate

The Cheetah

The cheetah
Who hunts for his prey
Agile, quick, predator
He is faster than a plane setting off
Like a bull when it sees red
I feel like the slowest thing in the world
It feels like a bullet going past my head
The cheetah
It makes me think of a car at high speed.

Adam Leach (10)
Woodlands Junior School, Harrogate

Clown Wanted

One clumsy clown
Who is rather tall
Wears bright hats
But not clever at all.

Who will get the crowd going
Who has chubby cheeks
Red hair, round nose
And able to speak.

Are you right
Or are you wrong?
If you're here
You can sing a song.

Come first now
And you'll have the job
At the circus
Contact Mr Bob.

Jennie Dunn (10)
Woodlands Junior School, Harrogate

Snakes

The killer snake
A killer
Slow, silky, strong
A giant moving stick
As slow as a snail
It makes me scared
It makes me feel like its prey
The killer snake
It makes me think of a king
Getting what he wants.

James Robinson (11)
Woodlands Junior School, Harrogate

Autumn Thoughts

Leaves falling on the ground
Spreading evenly all around
Lots of layers on the floor
Blown in through the doors

Squirrels run to gather acorns
Quickly before the day dawns
Red, orange all around
As the leaves touch the ground

The red and orange skies
Make my day
Because winter is on its way
And it was a happy autumn month!

Emma James (11)
Woodlands Junior School, Harrogate

Knights

Wanted!
A strong knight
Fierce and bold
You'll surely want to fight
In the freezing cold

Wielding a sword
Having some fun
You won't get bored
When you run, run, run!

Riding on your horse
A powerful, pointy sword
Jousting on the course
Time to kill the lord
Needed!

Craig Nelson (10)
Woodlands Junior School, Harrogate

Wizard Wonders

Wanted
One jolly wizard
With a long fuzzy beard
Robes of bright colours
A dazzling smile.

Wanted
A willing wizard
Expert in magical miracles
Owner of magnificent magic wand
Intelligent, reliable and responsible
Wanted!

Megan Simmon (10)
Woodlands Junior School, Harrogate

Blitz

I woke up suddenly from my bed,
With a throbbing pain in my head.
Thinking of the dreaded blackout,
From which I knew death was soon to spout.
From the enemy bomber planes,
With their killer rain.

I suddenly heard the siren,
Its moaning wail,
Sent fear through the hearts
Of everybody there.

Everybody is longing
For the bombing to cease
And the safe morning to come,
We don't want war, but peace.

Benjamin Pollard (10)
Woodlands Junior School, Harrogate

The Blitz

Walking out in the blackout
Pitch-black for the rest of the night
Shadows of lamp posts on the kerbs
Nothing is showing except white stripes.

'Ouch! Watch where you're going mate!'
People banging all around,
'Ooh, I'm sorry about that.'
While escaping to the shelters beneath the ground.

The siren screeches, 'Air raid! Air raid!'
Everyone scatters to the underground
As the droning vultures overhead
Are making a dreadful sound.

Everyone listens for the boom of the bombs
Anti-aircraft guns moan away
Mingled with chattering machine guns
Spitfires and Hurricanes make the enemy pay.

Liam Stephenson (11)
Woodlands Junior School, Harrogate

The Blackout!

'Lights out! Lights out!'
I heard the warden shout,
I went out to see,
What all the fuss was about.
'Get to the shelters! Get to the shelters!'
I heard the panicking people say,
A crowd ran towards me
And pushed me on my way.
I heard the sirens wailing,
The blackout has begun,
Should I find a place to hide?
Or should I go and run?

Thomas Clement (10)
Woodlands Junior School, Harrogate

Marching Off To War

In their heads they hear
The song their mother used to sing
As they march down the street
They say goodbye to everything

They march along the bumpy road
With sorrow in their hearts
Off to war they go
From their family they depart

Off to war they go
And may never be seen again
Storm clouds grow in the sky
And it begins to rain

They walk into the distance
And they vanish from our sight
They've gone to war to fight.

Stacey Marie Andrews (10)
Woodlands Junior School, Harrogate

Death Of A Life

This sad story starts with James,
He was only small,
He had no idea what happened next,
That severely shocked us all.

His mother was a good person,
No stealing, lies or cheating,
Did she really deserve to die,
In that terrible moment, so fleeting?

Now James is all alone,
With no one to hear him cry,
With no food or water running,
Why did his mother have to die?

Daniel Raymond (11)
Woodlands Junior School, Harrogate

The Knight

The knight waves to his lass at home
As he travels towards Blackburn
His spear as sharp as a bear's tooth
He returns two days later
With a blood-covered body on his saddle
And a mourning lass beside him.

Joshua Lindley (10)
Woodlands Junior School, Harrogate

Getting Told Off

Getting told off,
Your name is shouted out,
A shockwave goes through your body,
You feel self-conscious,
Everybody looks at you,
You tense all over,
Two minutes seems like an age,
It is over.

Sam Cremins (10)
Woodlands Junior School, Harrogate

The Marvellous Lion

The marvellous lion,
Chases his prey,
Running, pouncing, chasing,
Like the sun moving quickly,
Like the light of the world,
Its beauty makes my spine shiver,
Like I am powerless compared to the giant king,
The marvellous lion,
What would we do without his grace?

Lucy Collinge (10)
Woodlands Junior School, Harrogate

A Job At School

If you get this job
You will be the happiest person
On Earth.

The children are as good as gold
They will be the best class
You have ever had
In your life.

Do you have a kind heart
With a big smile?
Because if you do
This will be the job for you.

Apply now
Before the job has gone
At Woodlands Junior School, Harrogate.

Kym Croucher (10)
Woodlands Junior School, Harrogate

The Blackout!

The blackout! The blackout!
The blackout about.
'Lights out! Lights out!'
The warden shouts.
People falling in the pitch-black
As bombers fly and attack.

People shelter from the air raid
Loud screeching sounds were made
As the planes began to dive
We hope when it's over we've survived.

Lights, lights, lights are on
Children crying for their mums
We missed you lots
It's all over now.

Dominique Nicole Power (10)
Woodlands Junior School, Harrogate

There Is No Light

The sky is dark
There is no sound
The gas creeps silently
My friend has drowned.

The war is dreadful
Will I see my friends?
There is no glory
Only darkness descends.

No light ahead
To see us through darkness
All we have left
Is guns and markings.

There is no luck
The war's not at an end
We fight through the night
The silence is strained.

In the trenches I'm going insane
No lights, just darkness
Generals shouting, 'Attack right now!'
Give us a break, we're all worn out.

No light ahead
To see us through darkness
All we have left
Is guns and markings.

Barbed wire all around
No one can run, just get underground
The country life's all at risk
It's more than a game, remember this.

Jessica Watson (10)
Woodlands Junior School, Harrogate